AMERICAN GRUB

★ ★ ★ ★ ★ ★ ★

EATS
FOR KIDS
FROM
ALL
FIFTY STATES

Lynn Kuntz and
Jan Fleming

Illustrated by Mark A. Hicks

★ ★ ★ ★ ★ ★ ★

GIBBS
P
SMITH

Gibbs Smith, Publisher
Salt Lake City

07 06 05 04 03   5 4 3 2 1

Publishing History:

Published in 1997 by Scholastic, Inc.

Published in 2003 by

Gibbs Smith, Publisher
P.O. Box 667
Layton, Utah 84041

Orders: (1-800) 748-5439
www.gibbs-smith.com

Library of Congress Cataloging-in-Publication Data

Kuntz, Lynn, 1953-
American grub : eats for kids from all fifty states / Lynn Kuntz and Jan Fleming ; illustrated by Mark A. Hicks.
    p. cm.
Originally published: c1997.
Includes index.
Summary: Presents recipes from each of the fifty states, as well as providing background information on the states, particularly as it relates to their cuisine.
ISBN 1-58685-260-4
1. Cookery, American—Juvenile literature. 2. Food—Miscellanea—Juvenile literature. 3. United States—Miscellanea—Juvenile literature. [1. Cookery, American. 2. Food—Miscellanea. 3. United States—Miscellanea.] I. Fleming, Jan, 1958- II. Hicks, Mark A., ill. III. Title.

TX715.K936 2003
641.5973—dc21

2002030619

TO ARTIS, PIPER,
NICHOLAS, AND QUINN:
MY PARTNERS IN MANY
DELIGHTFULLY MESSY
BAKING PROJECTS!
L. K.

TO THE TASTERS:
CHASE AND KELLI. I HOPE
YOU HAVE AS MUCH FUN USING
THIS BOOK AS I HAVE HAD
PUTTING IT TOGETHER!
J. F.

CONTENTS

YOU ARE WHERE YOU EAT 6

READ THIS BEFORE YOU COOK! 8

HOME SAFE 10

STATES AND RECIPES

YOU ARE WHERE YOU EAT

If you come from Japan, your favorite food could be raw eel wrapped in seaweed. If you're French, you just might love eating snails. If you happen to visit China, your hostess might serve you cooked bear paws, but only as a treat on a special occasion.

The location, climate, soil, and terrain (mountainous or flat, for example) of a country greatly influence what the people who live there eat. Why? Because foods that are plentiful or grow well in a region are more likely to appear on local tables. Folks who live near the ocean, for instance, usually eat lots of fish and seafood. People who live inland eat meat from cattle, sheep, or game, depending on what kind of animals thrive on local grazing lands. People from mild climates with long growing seasons chow down lots of fruits and vegetables. People who live in cooler areas depend on hardy, cold-weather crops such as potatoes. You get the picture. With all that in mind, it's easy to see why people in different countries eat such different kinds of foods. But what about our own country? The United States has just about every kind of climate, soil, and terrain there is in the world, all within its own borders. It shouldn't be surprising, then, that different regions of the United States have many of their own unique foods.

In addition, our country was settled by people from all over the planet, who brought with them the cooking traditions of many an "old country." Lots of German, Hungarian, and Polish immigrants, for example, settled in the midwestern states. So it's easy to find foods such as blood sausage, kolbase, and headcheese in Ohio. Thousands of Chinese immigrants made their way to

California—so what state do you suppose has outstanding Chinese food? Ever lived in Texas? If so, your dinner table probably has had tacos, tamales, and enchiladas on it, spicy Texas favorites introduced by Texas' south-of-the-border neighbor, Mexico.

In this book, you'll find recipes for all kinds of foods that reflect the different climates, people, geography, and history of each of the fifty states. And you'll find out some fascinating food facts about the states themselves. With a little bit of help, you'll soon be cooking your way across the country—an expert in American grub!

READ THIS BEFORE YOU COOK!

Please ?

BEFORE YOU START:

✔ Always ask an adult's permission before beginning any project in the kitchen.

✔ Read through and discuss with an adult the safety tips in the Home Safe section immediately following this section.

GET READY:

Wash your hands with soap.

Push up your sleeves.

Tuck up loose clothing and long hair—you don't want them to drag in food or catch on fire!

Tie on an apron.

GET SET:
✔ Clear and clean sink and counter space so you have an uncluttered area in which to work.

✔ Read all the way through the recipe you've chosen, making sure you understand each and every step before you begin.

✔ Check to be sure you have all the ingredients the recipe calls for.

✔ Arrange all the ingredients and equipment (bowls, measuring spoons, pans, etc.) next to your working area.

GO!:
Now just follow the directions, one step at a time.

AT THE FINISH LINE:
Time to take a heaping serving of responsibility and leave the kitchen as nice as it was when you started (or even nicer!). This will earn big smiles (and invitations to cook again) from your parents.

✔ Rinse dirty bowls, pots, pans, and utensils as you finish with them. Then place them in a sink of soapy water to soak. You can wash or load them in the dishwasher all at once.

✔ Put each ingredient right back where you found it as soon as you finish with it. (This is especially important with refrigerated items.) Wipe off the outsides of containers (top, sides, and bottom). Make sure lids are right and tight.

✔ Clean spills on the floor as soon as they occur so no one will slip or fall.

✔ Clean electric mixers only after unplugging. Remove and wash beaters with soap and water. Clean mixer with damp cloth, but do not dunk in water.

✔ Ask for adult help when cleaning any appliance that has sharp blades (blenders and food processors, for instance).

HOME SAFE

The kitchen can be the warmest, liveliest, most inviting room in a house. It can also be very dangerous. Prizewinning chefs in the finest restaurants have help. So should you! Ask an adult to be your assistant.

The following tips will keep you and your assistant cooking safe:

ABOUT KNIVES:

✔ Don't handle sharp knives without your parents' permission.

✔ If you do use a sharp knife, keep your mind on what you're doing.

✔ Hold a sharp knife only by its handle—never by the blade.

✔ Always hold knives with the sharp side down.

✔ Cut away from yourself and away from anyone near you.

✔ Use knives only for cutting appropriate food.

✔ Never use a knife that's too big for you to comfortably handle.

✔ Cut on a cutting board. Never hold food to be chopped in your hand while you cut.

✔ When you walk with a knife, keep the point facing down.

✔ Never try to catch a falling knife.

✔ When not using knives, place them flat on the counter, back and out of the way.

✔ Never put a sharp knife into a sink to soak with dishes. (When you reach in for the dishes later, you might cut yourself.)

✔ Always place knives in the dishwasher or drainer with point down.

ABOUT THE STOVE TOP AND OVEN:

✔ Keep two hot-pad holders (oven mitts) next to the stove.

✔ Before turning on the oven, make sure rack is in middle position.

✔ Hold handles of pots and pans (using pot holders) when stirring ingredients (so pots and pans stay in place).

✔ Use dry hot-pad holders to handle hot pots, pans, and dishes. Hot surfaces will burn your hands right through wet hot pads.

✔ Never set a hot pot or pan on countertop. Set on trivet or unused burner.
✔ Boiling water is dangerous! Ask an adult to pour.
✔ Don't overfill pans with boiling liquid.
✔ Keep your face back and turned away when you lift the lid off a hot pot—the billowing steam can burn you.
✔ Place pots on the stove top with handles turned in (but not over another burner) to prevent someone from accidentally knocking them off.
✔ Use spoons with wooden or plastic handles to stir hot ingredients. (Metal spoons conduct heat and can burn your fingers.)
✔ Turn burners and oven off as soon as you finish with them.

ABOUT APPLIANCES:

✔ Don't use any appliance you're not familiar with.
✔ Never operate an appliance that's near the sink or sitting in water.
✔ If an appliance accidentally falls in water, do not reach in to remove it.
✔ Dry your hands thoroughly before plugging or unplugging appliances.
✔ Unplug mixer before inserting or removing beaters.
✔ Don't pull appliance cords to unplug. Pull the plug.
✔ Never open a blender or food processor while it's operating.
✔ Keep fingers away from the moving blades of electric mixers.

ABOUT THE MICROWAVE:

✔ Be sure you know what type of dishes can, and cannot, be used safely in the microwave.
✔ Have an adult review correct microwave procedures with you.
✔ If you can't comfortably reach a microwave, ask an adult to help. Never stand on a stool to operate.
✔ Don't stand in front of microwave while it's in operation.
✔ Use hot-pad holders to remove dishes from microwave.
✔ Keep your face back and turned away when you open covered dishes.

ABOUT COOKING WITH OIL

(which catches on fire easily):

✔ Never cook with oil unless an adult is assisting you.

✔ Use very little oil (a tablespoon or two at most) at a time.

✔ Never fry with oil at a high temperature.

✔ Never turn your back on frying oil.

✔ Never try to put out an oil fire with water. Water will make the fire splash and pop out of the pan. The adult assisting you can put it out by smothering it with a pan lid or pouring baking soda on it.

✔ Add food to hot oil slowly and carefully, keeping your face back and away (the oil can pop and burn you).

MISCELLANEOUS:

✔ Home alone: NOT a good time to cook.

✔ Don't grate your fingertips when you grate cheese!

✔ Be careful with lids of cans you've opened. Never touch the sharp, jagged edges. Throw away immediately.

✔ If something in a pot or pan catches fire, cover it with a lid to smother the fire—like you, a fire can't breathe without oxygen.

✔ If something in the oven or toaster oven catches fire, close the door and turn it off. The fire will die.

✔ Last but not least: Pets and small children are wonderful, but not in the kitchen when you're cooking! Make sure they're busy elsewhere.

When is a nut not a nut? When it's a peanut. Peanuts (also called goobers!) are actually legumes, closely related to the pea family. After a peanut plant's flowers wither, it grows stalks, called pegs, that reach into the ground. The ends of the pegs grow pods that contain seeds. When the seeds in the pods are mature, they can be dug up and eaten.

Peanuts are native to South America. Peanut plants were taken from there to Africa, and from Africa to North America during colonial days. More than two hundred thousand acres of Alabama land produce around six hundred million pounds of peanuts a year. They are sent all over the world.

Nickname: "Heart of Dixie"

Capital: Montgomery

ALABAMA

'BAMA BUTTER

What you need:

- 1 ½ cups unsalted roasted peanuts
- 1 tablespoon vegetable oil

What you do:

1. Set aside ¼ cup of peanuts (to be added later to make the peanut butter chunky).

2. In a food processor, mix the remaining 1 ¼ cups of peanuts and the oil together until smooth.

3. Stir in the ¼ cup of peanuts that you set aside.

4. Spread your peanut butter with a dull knife on apple wedges or celery. Keep your homemade peanut butter in a sealed container in the refrigerator for up to 2 weeks.

Makes 1 cup

NUTTY PUTTY

What you need:

- 3 ½ cups peanut butter
- 4 cups powdered sugar
- 3 ½ cups corn syrup or honey
- 4 cups dried milk powder

What you do:

1. In a large bowl, mix all ingredients together.

2. Divide into 10–15 portions.

3. Store any extra portions in sealable plastic bags in the refrigerator or freezer.

4. Use this treat as fun dough. With clean hands, mold and shape the putty into animals, flowers, and other objects and when you're done, eat them, too!

A famous American scientist named George Washington Carver developed 300 ways to use the peanut plant. These include printer's ink, rubbing oil, rubber, gasoline and, of course, peanut butter.

Hey, who are you calling a goober?!

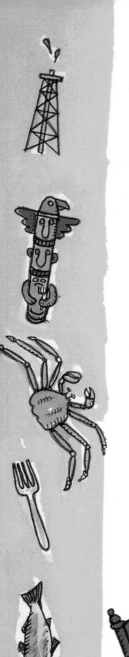

Alaskans catch more fish than fisherfolk from any other state—about $3 billion worth every year. Half of that fish is salmon. Some of it is shipped fresh to fine restaurants all over the world. It may also be frozen, smoked, or canned before going to market.

Nickname: "The Last Frontier"

Capital: Juneau

ALASKA

NORTHWEST SALMON SANDWICHES

What you need:
- ½ cup onion, chopped
- ¼ cup butter
- 2 eggs, beaten
- ¼ cup parsley, chopped
- 1 teaspoon dry mustard
- ½ teaspoon salt
- 16 ounces canned salmon
- ⅓ cup dry bread crumbs
- 1 cup oil for frying
- 6 hamburger buns, buttered

What you do:

1. In a small frying pan, cook the onion in the butter until tender.

2. In a large bowl, combine the onion, eggs, parsley, dry mustard, salt, and salmon together and mix well.

3. With your hands, divide the mixture into 6 equal parts and shape each part into a salmon patty (a burger-shaped circle).

4. Put the bread crumbs on a small plate and roll each salmon patty in them.

5. Heat the oil in a large frying pan on medium-high heat and carefully place the patties into the pan with a spatula.

6. Cook until bottom sides are brown, then turn over and brown the other sides.

7. Warm the buns by placing them, buttered side up, on a cookie sheet in the oven on broil for several seconds. Place salmon burgers between warmed buns spread with mayonnaise or mustard.

Sandwiches were invented more than two hundred years ago. Here's the story: an Englishman named John Montagu, the Earl of Sandwich, liked card games so much that he never wanted to stop playing long enough to eat. One day he came up with the idea of having his roasted meat served between two slices of bread. That way, he could eat with one hand, hold his cards in the other, and keep right on playing!

The largest Native American tribe in the United States, the Navajo nation, lives in Arizona, New Mexico, and Utah, on a reservation that covers fourteen million acres—an area about the size of the state of West Virginia. The Navajo are a proud tribe who carry on many traditions from the past: speaking the language of their ancestors, herding their sheep across beautiful, high desert lands, and weaving blankets and rugs from their wool. Navajo fry bread is a fairly new (twentieth-century) Navajo tradition.

Nickname: "Grand Canyon State"

Capital: Phoenix

ARIZONA

POWWOW WOW BREAD

What you need:
- 4 cups flour (Bluebird works best)
- 1 tablespoon baking powder
- 1 teaspoon salt
- 1 ½ cups water
- 1 handful of powdered milk
- 2 cups vegetable oil for frying

What you do:
1. In a large bowl, mix the flour, baking powder, and salt.

2. Add the water and the powdered milk to the flour mixture. Mix together with your hands until it's not sticky. You can add more water if it's too dry, or add more flour if it's too sticky.

3. With your hands, mold the fry bread into flat circles, each about 6 inches across. Put a hole in the middle of the dough with your finger.

4. Heat the oil (it should be about 1 inch deep) in a large frying pan on high heat. Cook the fry bread until it is golden brown on both sides.

Ask an adult for help, and be careful—the oil is hot!

5. Remove the bread from the oil with tongs and set on paper towels to drain the oil from the fry bread.

Put your choice of cooked ground beef or chicken, grated cheddar or Monterey Jack cheese, shredded lettuce, and diced tomatoes on top of the fry bread. (Be inventive, too—what other toppings might be good on a Navajo taco?)

Serves 4–6

Navajo fry bread is so popular throughout the Southwest that it's sold at fairs, festivals, school carnivals, flea markets, athletic events, malls, and even powwows.

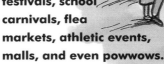

ARKANSAS

Arkansas is the "Watermelon Capital of the World." The town of Hope is known for growing whopper watermelons weighing in at over two hundred pounds. (Hope's world-record holder tipped the scales at a juicy 260 pounds!) Every year, on the third weekend in August, Hope hosts the Annual Watermelon Festival. Activities include watermelon-eating contests, seed-spitting contests (resist the temptation to try this indoors!), and watermelon tennis and chess tournaments.

Nickname: "Land of Opportunity"

Capital: Little Rock

Watermelon tastes wonderful when it's simply chilled and sliced. But Arkansas folks know how to dress it up and make it positively elegant! Here are some ways watermelon is eaten in Arkansas: watermelon rind pie, watermelon muffins, watermelon cream pie, watermelon ice cream, watermelon sherbet, watermelon soup, watermelon cake with watermelon icing, watermelon fondue, watermelon glazed ham, watermelon cookies, and sauteed watermelon rind! Though there's no sure way to pick a perfect watermelon, here are some tips: Look for a firm, symmetrical shape and a dull, rather than shiny, surface with no bruises or dents. The underside of a ripe melon should be yellowish. How sweet a watermelon is depends mainly on what variety it is.

WATERMELON FRAPPÉ

What you need:
- 4 cups diced watermelon, without seeds
- 2 tablespoons lemon juice
- 1 teaspoon lemon rind, grated
- 1 bottle (12 ounces) ginger ale

What you do:
1. Put the first 3 ingredients into blender and whirl until frothy.
2. Pour mixture into a pitcher.
3. Add ginger ale to the pitcher and stir.
4. Pour into tall glasses filled with ice cubes.

Makes about 5 cups

W hat do Californians eat? Just about everything! California is home to people from hundreds of ethnic groups, who eat special foods from all over the world.

One of the largest ethnic groups in California is made up of people of Chinese ancestry. In fact, San Francisco's Chinatown, with its colorful restaurants and shops topped by pagoda-style roofs, is one of the largest Chinese communities in the world outside of Asia.

Dragons play an important part in many Chinese traditions. In San Francisco, a traditional Chinese New Year's Day parade always includes a group of people wearing a large dragon costume, dancing through the streets.

Because dragons mean good luck and wealth, they're welcome in many forms—decorations, food, costumed characters, etc.—during Chinese New Year celebrations.

CALIFORNIA

Nickname: "Golden State"

Capital: Sacramento

CHINATOWN DRAGON CAKES

What you need:

- ½ cup butter, softened
- ¼ cup sugar
- 1 egg yolk (carefully separated from the white part)
- 1 cup flour
- 1 cup strawberry jam

What you do:

1. Preheat oven to 375 degrees.
2. In a large mixing bowl, combine the softened butter, sugar, and egg yolk, and mix well.
3. Add flour and mix until it looks like cookie dough. Form the dough into a large ball and wrap it in aluminum foil. Put the wrapped ball in the refrigerator for 30 minutes.
4. Unwrap the chilled dough and make little balls the size of golf balls.
5. With your thumb, gently make a hole in the small balls and fill each with a half teaspoon of strawberry jam.
6. Cover cookie sheets with aluminum foil and place each dragon cake on the cookie sheet. Bake for 20 minutes or until golden brown. **Makes 24**

COLORADO

Imagine a large group of families walking away from their homes one day, never to return. Imagine them leaving clothes, bedding, cooking utensils, dishes, tools, weapons, even the children's toys and games behind.

Imagine that six hundred years later, a couple of cowboys, rounding up stray cattle, stumble upon the homes, eerie and hushed, still littered with the families' abandoned belongings.

There is such a town, built in a dry, protected hollow in the cliffs of southwestern Colorado. Who were the families who once lived there? Why did they walk away, never to return?

No one knows for sure. We don't even know what they called themselves. Today they're called Anasazi, "the ancient ones." From around A.D. 1100 until about A.D. 1300, they built dozens of multistoried brick villages in southwestern Colorado in an area called Mesa Verde. You can visit the remains of many of those villages today.

The Anasazi were the Southwest's earliest farmers. They grew beans, squash, and melons, and raised turkeys to eat on special feast days. But their most important crop was corn. They paid tribute to it in dances, stories, songs, celebrations, and ceremonies.

ANASAZI BEAN DIP & CORNY TORTILLAS

ANASAZI BEAN DIP

What you need:

- 2 cans pinto beans
- 1 medium onion, chopped
- 1 teaspoon garlic, chopped
- 1 teaspoon cumin
- ½ teaspoon each salt and pepper
- 1 cup sour cream*
- 1 cup salsa

*Note: The Anasazi didn't have sour cream, but we added it to make your dip extra tasty.

What you do:

1. Drain the liquid from the beans. Put beans in food processor or blender and puree them for 3 seconds. Add the remaining ingredients except for sour cream and salsa. Puree until the mixture is well blended.

2. Pour mixture into a medium bowl and mix in sour cream and salsa. Stir thoroughly.

3. Pour dip into bowl and serve with whole, warm Anasazi corn tortillas or baked corn tortilla chips.

CORNY TORTILLAS

What you need:

- 2 cups cornmeal
  (Masa Harina works best)
- 1 ½ cups warm water
- ¼ teaspoon salt

What you do:

1. In a medium bowl, mix together cornmeal, water, and salt until dough isn't sticky. (If it's too sticky, add more cornmeal; if it's too dry, add more water.)

2. Form dough into golf-ball-sized balls and pat with your hands to form paper-thin, 6-inch rounds. Place tortilla on hot, lightly oiled griddle and cook until brown. (Your tortilla isn't crispy yet, but you can still eat it. Spoon some dip on it and then roll the tortilla up to eat it!)

3. Preheat the oven to 350 degrees.

4. Place the cooked tortillas on a cookie sheet and brush each one with oil. Then cut them into strips with a pizza cutter.

5. Bake for about 5-10 minutes or until crispy.

6. Once the chips have cooled a bit, dip them into the Anasazi bean dip and enjoy!

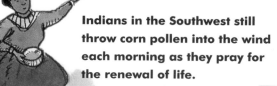

Indians in the Southwest still throw corn pollen into the wind each morning as they pray for the renewal of life.

Connecticut's cool, clean, nutrient-rich coastal waters produce hundreds of thousands of bushels of clams each year. So it's not surprising that Connecticut is famous for delicious clam chowder. Don't confuse Connecticut's New-England style chowder, made with milk or cream, with Manhattan's version. Many Connecticut old-timers turn up their noses at tomato-based Manhattan clam chowder, saying it's just vegetable soup with clams added! But don't let them kid you—although thick, creamy chowder is the favorite in Connecticut, both kinds are popular.

Nickname: "The Constitution State"

Capital: Hartford

CONNECTICUT

DREAMY CREAMY CLAM CHOWDER

What you need:

- (4) 5-ounce cans clams, drained
- 1 bunch green onions, chopped
- 3 medium-sized potatoes, cut into cubes
- 1 can corn, drained
- 1 ½ cups water
- 1 ½ teaspoons salt
- ¼ teaspoon pepper
- (1) 13-ounce can evaporated milk

What you do:

1. Put the drained clams into a large saucepan on medium-high heat. Add green onions, potatoes, and corn.

2. Add the water, salt, and pepper.

3. Cover and bring to a boil, then turn the heat to low and simmer for 30 minutes. (The potatoes should be tender.)

4. While the soup is simmering, add the evaporated milk and stir. Heat through.

5. Pour soup into small bowls and serve with little oyster crackers.

The word chowder comes from *chudiere,* the French word for a cauldron, or cooking pot.

Although clams are native to both sides of the Atlantic Ocean, the first white people to taste them were Europeans who settled in America. Native Americans, whose ancestors had been eating clams thousands of years ago, taught the settlers how delicious and nutritious clams could be. The Indians used the clam shells for utensils, jewelry, and money.

Manhattan!

New England!

Each autumn, thousands of people flock to the town of Lewes, Delaware, for The World *Whoooooooaughhhh* Championship Punkin' Chunkin', one of the world's liveliest pumpkin festivals. Men, women, boys, and girls in Lewes spend weeks devising elaborate contraptions (slingshots, catapults, even cannons) capable of hurling fat, orange pumpkins long distances. Why? Because the "pilot" of the farthest-flung pumpkin receives a first-place prize of $2,500! The farthest pumpkin flight yet recorded? More than half a mile!

Pumpkins are members of the gourd family, along with watermelons, cantaloupes, cucumbers, and a large variety of squashes. They originated in the New World, possibly as long ago as 5000 B.C. Native Americans taught European settlers how to make soups, puddings, bread, pancakes, and even beer from the all-American pumpkin flesh and seeds!

Nickname: "First State"

Capital: Dover

DELAWARE

PUNKIN' CHUNKIN' CHEESECAKE
What you need:

- 1 prepared graham-cracker pie crust
- ¾ cup canned pumpkin
- ¾ cup sugar
- 3 egg yolks (carefully separated from the white parts)

- 1 tablespoon cinnamon
- ½ teaspoon nutmeg
- ½ teaspoon ginger
- ¼ teaspoon salt
- (3) 8-ounce packages cream cheese, softened
- 1/4 cup plus 2 tablespoons sugar
- 1 egg plus 1 egg yolk
- 2 tablespoons whipping cream
- 1 tablespoon cornstarch
- ½ teaspoon lemon extract
- ½ teaspoon vanilla extract

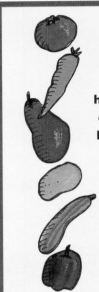

What's the difference between a vegetable and a fruit? The part of the plant that holds the seed(s) is always a fruit—cucumbers, beans, squash, pumpkins, peppers, eggplant, tomatoes, and avocados, for instance. All other parts of a plant (root, stems, etc.) are vegetables.

6. Pour into the prepared graham cracker pan.

7. Bake for 50–55 minutes. Using oven mitts, remove the pan from the oven and cool on a wire rack. (The center will be soft but will firm up after it is chilled.) Chill in refrigerator for 4 hours.

Serves 6–8

American kids started making Halloween jack-o-lanterns out of pumpkins in the 1840s, when Irish immigrants introduced the custom of carving faces from turnips for All Hallow's Eve, an ancient Celtic celebration highlighting the turning of the year.

What you do:

1. Preheat oven to 350 degrees.

2. In a medium bowl, combine pumpkin, ¾ cup sugar, 3 egg yolks, cinnamon, nutmeg, ginger, and salt. Mix well with electric beaters and set aside.

3. In a large mixing bowl, beat the cream cheese with an electric mixer until light and fluffy. Gradually add 1/4 cup plus 2 tablespoons of sugar and mix well.

4. Add the egg, egg yolk, and whipping cream and beat well. Add the cornstarch and extracts and beat until mixture is smooth.

5. Add the pumpkin mixture to the cream cheese mixture and mix well.

Oranges have been cultivated (planted and cared for) in China, Japan, and India for thousands of years. During the fifteenth and sixteenth centuries, Portuguese who explored the Far East took orange trees back to Europe. From there they were taken to America. Florida's warm, sunny climate is so ideal for growing oranges that Florida is now the world's leading supplier of oranges.

Fifty pounds of juice can be squeezed from 100 pounds of oranges.

Nickname: "Sunshine State"

Capital: Tallahassee

FLORIDA

SUNSHINE JUICE

What you need:

- 8 Florida juice oranges
- Handheld juicer
- Strainer

What you do:

1. Using a sharp knife, carefully slice the oranges in half.

2. Either by hand or with the juicer, squeeze the juice from the orange into a bowl.

3. Pour the juice through the strainer into a glass. The strainer will collect all of the seeds and pulp that you squeezed out.

The orange juice will taste very sweet. You can add ice cubes to your juice, or you can refrigerate your oranges before you squeeze them and the juice will already be cold.

As early as the 1760s, oranges and orange juice, sealed in barrels, were shipped from Florida to Europe.

Four out of every five glasses of orange juice Americans drink come from oranges grown in Florida.

Georgia is called the Peach State, not only because so many peaches are grown there (almost 180 million pounds a year!), but because peaches have been grown in Georgia since colonial days, before the United States was a country or Georgia a state. By 1857, two hundred varieties of peach trees were grown in Georgia. In fact, today the most famous street in Georgia is Atlanta's Peachtree Street.

Nickname: "Peach State"

Capital: Atlanta

GEORGIA

PEACHES SUNNY-SIDE UP

What you need:

- 10 ounces vanilla yogurt
- 2 tablespoons sugar
- 2 graham crackers, halved
- 1 small can of peach halves, or
      1 fresh peach, peeled and halved
- ½ teaspoon cinnamon

What you do:

1. Mix yogurt and sugar together in a small bowl.

2. Place half a graham cracker on the center of a plate. Spoon the yogurt mixture on top of the cracker and the plate so that it covers the cracker completely.

3. Put a peach half, rounded part facing up, in the middle of the yogurt. Sprinkle a little cinnamon over it. It should look like a sunny-side-up egg!

Serves 2

The Reverend Sylvester Graham would certainly have been surprised to see how popular graham crackers, made from the finely ground, whole-wheat flour he "invented" more than one hundred and fifty years ago, have become. Graham was a doctor who wanted to improve the health of Americans by getting them to cook with more nutritious foods.

When people think of Hawaii, they usually think of pineapples, one of this state's most important and delicious exports! The pineapple, which was given its name because it looks something like a pinecone, is really a group of tightly packed small fruits. Pineapples can weigh from 4 to 20 pounds. Each year, thousands of tourists who visit Hawaii return to their families and friends with gifts of fresh Hawaiian pineapples. Most canned pineapple sold in the United States is grown in Hawaii.

Nickname: "Aloha State"

Capital: Honolulu

HAWAII

HOW TO PEEL AND CUT A FRESH PINEAPPLE

1. Slice off the pineapple's top and bottom with a sharp knife.
2. Stand the pineapple on its base (bottom) and peel away the skin, from top to bottom, in long, vertical strips.
3. Cut out the 'eyes' with a paring knife.
4. Cut pineapple into quarters from the top down.
5. Cut core from the center of each quarter.

Just how do you peel this thing?

ALOHA-BOBS
What you need:
- 12 fresh strawberries, washed
- 1 cup pineapple chunks
- 12 seedless grapes, red or green, washed
- 2 bananas, peeled and sliced into 1-inch pieces
- 6 skewers

What you do:
1. Carefully cut the stems off the strawberries with a knife.
2. Build your kabob by pushing one piece of each fruit at a time onto the skewer in any order you like.

Serve as a side dish with breakfast, lunch, or dinner. It can be a snack or a dessert too.

Makes 6 kabobs

25

IDAHO

When Americans were recently asked what came to mind when they heard the word *potato,* 82 percent said: Idaho!

Farmers in South America first began cultivating wild potatoes more than three thousand years ago. Spanish explorers took them back to Europe. At first Europeans couldn't get used to the idea of eating the underground part of a plant, so they ate the leaves instead. Too bad! The leaves made them sick! From Europe potatoes were taken to England and Ireland. Potatoes became the most important food in Ireland, and millions of Irish people died of starvation when a plant disease destroyed Ireland's potato crop in 1845. Millions more sold everything they owned and moved to the United States.

Potatoes were first grown in North America in 1719 but became increasingly important as thousands of potato-loving Irish and Europeans immigrated. The first potato farmer in Idaho was actually not a farmer at all but a Presbyterian missionary. He went to Idaho in 1836 to spread Christianity among the Nez Perce Indians. He also taught them how to grow potatoes so they wouldn't have to depend entirely on hunting and gathering for food. However, he left after just two years, when the Indians attacked a neighboring missionary's family. That was the end of Idaho potatoes until 1860, when a group of Mormon pioneers moved from Utah into southern Idaho. They grew thirty-three bushels of potatoes in Idaho's rich volcanic soil the first year. Sixteen years later they and their Mormon neighbors shipped more than 2.5 million pounds of potatoes to mining camps as far away as California. Today Idaho produces almost 30 percent of all the potatoes in the United States.

The French call potatoes *pommes de terre,* which means "apples of the earth." The Irish call them *praties.* Americans sometimes call them "spuds."

26

On September 19, 1992, at the 64th annual Idaho Spud Day celebrations held in Shelley, Idaho, five women with standard kitchen knives peeled 1,064 pounds, 6 ounces of potatoes in 45 minutes! Spud Day events include a tug-of-war over a moat of mashed potatoes (mixed in a cement truck!).

Idaho license plates proudly display the words "Famous Potatoes."

CHEESY SPUDS

What you need:

- 4 medium baking potatoes, washed
- ¼ pound cheddar cheese, grated
- ¼ cup plain yogurt
- 2 teaspoons green onions, chopped
- 2 tablespoons butter

What you do:

1. Prick each of the potatoes with a fork several times.

2. Fold a white paper towel in the microwave oven. Put the potatoes on the paper towel in a circle.

3. Microwave the potatoes on high power for 12–15 minutes. When you pinch them (carefully—they're hot!), they should still be a little firm. Set them aside for about 10 minutes.

4. While you are cooking the potatoes, mix the remaining ingredients together.

5. Cut the potatoes in half lengthwise and scoop out the potato. Mix the potato into the cheese mixture and spoon the new potato-cheese mixture back into the skins.

6. Microwave again for about 2 minutes on high power to reheat.

Serves 8

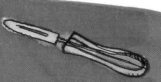

I n 1942 Ike Sewell of Chicago layered handfuls of cheese, tomatoes, sausage, pepperoni, mushrooms, broccoli, peppers, olives, anchovies, and MORE on an extra-thick pizza dough. His idea was to create a pizza that customers at his Pizzeria Uno restaurant could make a one-dish meal of. What did he call it? Chicago Deep-dish Pizza! People loved his fat pizzas so much that deep-dish pizza is now popular all over the world.

Although our recipe is not Sewell's recipe (that's a well-guarded secret), it's delicious!

Nickname: "Land of Lincoln"

Capital: Springfield

ILLINOIS

DEEP-DISH PIZZA PIE
What you need:
- Deep-dish pizza pan

Dough:
- 1 package yeast
- ¾ cups warm water
- 2 cups flour
- 5 tablespoons olive oil
- 2 teaspoons sugar

The word *pizza* is Italian for pie.

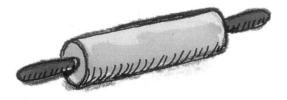

Toppings:
- 1 cup tomato sauce
- 1 cup shredded mozzarella cheese
- Additional choices: sliced mushrooms, black olives, green peppers, pineapple, onions, sliced pepperoni, etc.

What you do:
1. Preheat oven to 425 degrees.

2. In a medium-sized bowl, mix the yeast and water. Wait about 10 minutes and then add the rest of the ingredients. Mix well. Knead (press and push) the dough with your hands for about 10 minutes.

3. Place the dough into a round, oiled bowl and cover it with a cloth. Set it in a warm place for 1 hour.

4. On a surface lightly sprinkled with flour, roll the dough out into a big enough circle to fit the pan. Brush the pan with oil. Put the dough in the pan, pushing it up the sides of the pan. The dough should be about ½-inch thick at the bottom and ¾-inch thick on the sides. Brush the top of the dough with oil.

5. Set the pan aside for about 25 minutes so that the dough can rise a little more.

6. Put shredded cheese on top of the dough and then layer with tomato sauce and the toppings of your choice. Another layer of shredded cheese should end up on the top of your pizza.

7. Bake for 35 minutes or until cheese bubbles and browns. Carefully cut into wedges and serve.

Deep-dish pizza dough, like regular bread dough, requires only a few ingredients: flour, water, salt, sugar, oil, and yeast. Yeast is a fungus. It feeds on sugar, then releases carbon dioxide gas. The gas trapped in the dough makes it puff up, or "rise." After the dough is baked, it's full of tiny holes where the gas bubbles were. This is what makes deep-dish pizza dough so light.

You may know that Indiana is called the "Crossroads of America" because of its central location. What you might not know is that Indiana is home to some of the largest Old-Order Amish communities in the country.

The Amish are a very strict religious sect (group) who live separately from the rest of the world. They live very simple farming lives and use no electricity—no radios, TVs, electric lights, washing machines, telephones, cars, not even farm equipment with motors.

The men and boys wear dark, old-fashioned clothes and wide-brimmed hats, and the women and girls wear long dresses and bonnets.

The Amish are considered some of the finest farmers in America. Amish women are wonderful cooks, preparing everything from scratch (no cans, mixes, or appliances) with fruits, vegetables, and meats that are grown on their own farms.

Nickname: "Hoosiers"

Capital: Indianapolis

INDIANA

BACK-TO-BASICS BRUNCH

What you need:
- 4 eggs
- 2 cups milk
- ½ teaspoon salt
- ¼ teaspoon dry mustard
- ⅛ teaspoon onion salt
- Bacon or sausage, cooked and crumbled
- 2 cups toasted bread croutons (you can use packaged croutons)
- 1 cup cheddar cheese, grated

What you do:
1. Preheat oven to 325 degrees.
2. Grease an 11 x 7-inch casserole dish.
3. In a medium bowl, beat eggs, milk, and seasonings with a wooden spoon.
4. Crumble bacon or sausage into the mixture.
5. Put croutons on the bottom of the casserole dish.
6. Sprinkle the cheese over the croutons and then pour the egg mixture over the cheese.
7. Bake for 50 minutes.
8. Using oven mitts, take the casserole dish out of the oven and set on top of the stove. Let cool about 5 minutes, then cut into squares and serve.

Serves 4 or more

Corn grew only in our hemisphere until Columbus took it back to Spain. From there it was taken around the world. Iowa, a major part of the "Corn Belt" (a fertile region made up of eight states in the central United States that is largely devoted to growing corn), is one of the top corn producers in the country.

Many of the early white settlers in North America would have died if the Indians hadn't shared their corn and shown the settlers how to plant and care for their own. Corn was so highly prized in the early pioneering days that settlers often used it instead of money, trading it with the Indians for furs.

IOWA

Nickname: "Hawkeye State"

Capital: Des Moines

POPZACORN BALLS

What you need:
- 1 ½ tablespoons butter
- 1 ½ cups brown sugar
- 6 tablespoons water
- Candy thermometer
- 6 cups popped corn

What you do:

1. In a medium saucepan on high heat, combine butter, sugar, and water. Stir together until sugar is dissolved. Bring to a boil.

2. Cover and cook on low for about 3 minutes, then uncover and cook without stirring until the candy thermometer reads 238 degrees.

3. Pour sauce over the popped corn and stir gently with a wooden spoon until the popcorn is coated well.

4. When mixture is cool enough to touch, butter your fingers and form the popcorn into balls or other shapes you like. You can insert a popsicle stick into your shape so it's easier to hold while you eat.

Note: While you are cooking the mixture, you can add food coloring to make colorful popcorn balls.

WHAT MAKES POP-CORN POP?

A popcorn kernel is the seed of a corn plant. Moisture sealed inside the kernel helps keep it alive until conditions are right for it to sprout. When the kernel is heated very rapidly, the moisture inside turns to steam. The pressure from the expanding steam bursts the kernel open, and the corn inside pops out!

Early explorers thought Kansas was a desert that would never be suitable for agriculture. But the hardworking immigrants who settled in Kansas were convinced they could turn the fertile, well-drained soil into productive farmland. Instead of giving up during years when it was so hot, cold, rainy, or dry that many of their crops died, those persistent (stick-with-it) Kansas farmers developed crops that could survive and thrive in Kansas' unpredictable climate.

They discovered that sunflowers, which can survive long "dry spells" (week after week with no rain) are well-suited to conditions in parts of Kansas where it rains less than twenty inches a year. The seeds are rich in protein and delicious when roasted and salted. Thanks to those hardworking Kansas farmers, Kansas sunflower seeds—about 338 million pounds of them every year—now feed hungry people (and birds, too) all over the world.

> **Some sunflowers grow up to a foot in diameter and produce up to a thousand seeds per flower!**

Nickname: "Sunflower State"

Capital: Topeka

KANSAS

CRUNCHY SUNFLOWER CEREAL

What you need:

- 2 cups sunflower-seed kernels
- 2 cups quick oatmeal
- ½ cup cashew pieces
- ½ cup almonds
- ½ cup shredded coconut
- ½ cup vegetable oil
- ½ cup honey
- ¼ cup molasses

What you do:

1. Preheat oven to 300 degrees.
2. In a large bowl, combine all ingredients. Use your hands and mix well.
3. Spread onto a shallow baking pan.
4. Bake for 15 minutes. Carefully remove from oven with hot pads, stir mixture, and then bake for 10 minutes more. Let cool. Store in tightly sealed container or sealable plastic bag.

Sunflowers were growing wild in Kansas long before white people arrived. Because they are native to our country, sunflower seeds are truly an all-American food.

People all over the world think of Kentucky when they think of fried chicken. Why? Because Kentucky's Colonel Harland Sanders (the guy with the white suit, string tie, and goatee) started a fried-chicken business that became the world's largest international restaurant chain, with yearly sales of $5.4 billion. Here's the story:

Back in the 1930s, Colonel Sanders, who had recently opened one of Kentucky's first motels, decided to open a cafe and sell fried chicken (already a favorite food of Kentuckians) made with his "secret recipe." To convince people who ate at the cafe to stay at his motel, he constructed a fully furnished motel room in the cafe that customers had to walk through on the way to the rest room.

Colonel Sanders' original cafe in Corbin, Kentucky, was the world's first fast-food restaurant. It's now a working museum (in other words, they're still frying chicken!) that looks exactly as it did when Colonel Sanders opened for business that first day.

Nickname: "Bluegrass State"

Capital: Frankfort

KENTUCKY

Although the recipe given here is not Colonel Sanders' secret recipe (it wouldn't be a secret if we knew it!), it's delicious.

TOP SECRET

FINGER-LICKIN' CHICKEN

What you need:
- 1 teaspoon shortening
- ½ cup flour
- ½ teaspoon paprika
- ½ teaspoon salt
- 8 chicken pieces

What you do:

1. Preheat oven to 425 degrees. Grease a baking pan, 13 x 9 x 2 inches, with shortening.

2. Put the flour, paprika, and salt in a large sealable plastic bag and close it tightly. Shake it well to mix the ingredients.

3. Put 2 or 3 chicken pieces in the bag. Close it tightly again and shake the bag so the chicken is covered with the flour mixture. Repeat this until you have coated all of the chicken pieces. Place them side by side in the baking pan with the skin sides facing up.

4. Bake for 55 minutes, or until the chicken is golden brown on the outside.

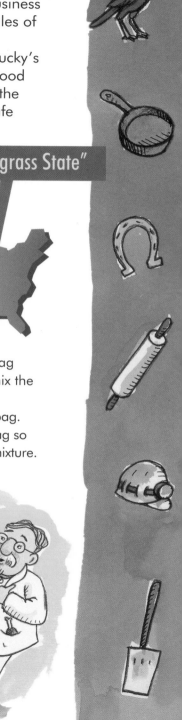

Serves 4

Louisiana is famous for jazz music, Mardi Gras (an elaborate, yearly festival that includes wearing costumes with masks and attending lots of parades and special events), gracious Southern plantations, alligators, and Cajun food. What's Cajun food? It's old-fashioned, down-home, French-country cooking, well seasoned with local Louisiana spices (including plenty of hot peppers!). The Cajuns who live in Louisiana today are descendants of Acadians (French colonists who left Nova Scotia, Canada, for Louisiana in the 1700s).

Wherever you go in southern Louisiana, you'll find an entire menu of unique Cajun dishes that aren't available in any other state. Cajuns are fond of saying they "live to eat," rather than the other way around!

Nickname: "Pelican State"

Capital: Baton Rouge

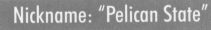

LOUISIANA

DOWN-ON-THE-BAYOU GUMBO

What you need:
- 1 three-pound bag chicken pieces, washed
- 12 cups water
- 4 tablespoons butter
- ½ cup flour

- 1 medium green bell pepper, chopped
- 1 ½ pounds okra, sliced
- (1) 16-ounce can stewed tomatoes, chopped
- 2 celery stalks, chopped
- 1 medium onion, diced
- 1 teaspoon each of salt and pepper

ALLÔ! (HELLO!)

Many Cajuns still speak a unique blend of French and English.

What you do:

1. Put the water into a large pot and add the chicken. Cook uncovered on medium heat until chicken is tender (about 1 hour).

2. Drain the liquid into a large bowl and save this broth. Set the chicken aside to cool.

3. Take the skin off the chicken, remove the bones, and tear the chicken into small, bite-sized pieces. You may need an adult to help you with this step.

4. In a large saucepan, melt the butter on medium-low heat and stir in the flour. Cook until the mixture is a light brown. Stir constantly.

5. Add the vegetables and the chicken broth and cook until the vegetables are tender and the sauce thickens (approximately 30 minutes).

6. Add the chicken and salt and pepper. Serve hot and enjoy!

Serves 8

The word *gumbo* comes from an African word meaning okra. If you're not excited about okra, you can make your gumbo without it. Also, Louisianians usually add a thickening powder to gumbo called *filé*, which is made from the dried leaves of a sassafras plant.

We chose hard-rock candy for Maine's recipe to commemorate (remember) this state's 228 miles of rugged, hard-rock Atlantic shoreline.

A few words about candy: People have liked sweet treats from the beginning of written history, when the Egyptians first made candy from honey mixed with seeds and fruits. Thousands of years later, people in India learned to crush stalks of sugarcane and boil the juicy pulp to evaporate the water, leaving a dark brown sugar. Knowledge of sugarmaking gradually spread through the Orient and, eventually, the Middle East. But it was not until the eleventh century that Western civilization tasted sugar.

Of course everyone in the Western world loved it! At first only the very wealthiest people could afford sugar, but as more and more sugarcane was cultivated, both in Europe and later in the New World, sugar became something everyone could afford. Serious candymaking for profit began in England, but it was in America that it became a big business. (Americans eat about 20 pounds of candy apiece every year!)

Unfortunately, sugar is bad for your teeth. But most experts agree that eating sugar is not the problem—letting it remain in the mouth is. The bacteria that cause tooth decay multiply quickly in sticky food particles that get trapped in the tiny spaces between your teeth. If you brush your teeth immediately after you eat candy or drink sugary drinks, you can enjoy them—as long as you don't overdo!

Nickname: "Pine Tree State"

Capital: Augusta

MAINE

HARD-ROCK CANDY

What you need:

- 4 cups sugar
- (1) 1-quart canning jar, large-mouthed
- 3 ½ cups boiling water
- 1 dull knife
- 1 metal weight (paper clip or washer)
- 1 piece of clean white string,
     8 inches long
- 1 pencil

What you do:

1. Pour the sugar into the jar. Then slowly pour the boiling water into the jar. Dip the knife into the water to the bottom, and stir well. Keep adding the hot water slowly and stir until all of the sugar is dissolved.

2. Tie the weight to one end of the string, then tie the other end of the string to the pencil.

3. Put the pencil across the top of the jar. Roll the string around the pencil until the weight is almost touching the bottom of the jar.

4. Put the uncovered jar in a warm place and leave it alone for 2 or 3 days.

5. Crystals will start growing on the string, on the jar, and also on the surface of the sugar

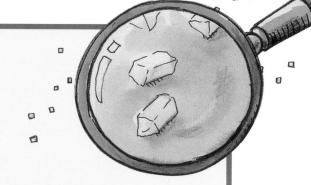

Examine a grain of table sugar through a powerful magnifying glass. When these tiny sugar crystals are heated and allowed to cool again, a chemical reaction takes place and the sugar crystallizes.

solution. Break up the crust each day so that the water can evaporate. When the water evaporates from the jar, more crystals will grow.

6. When all the water has evaporated, you can eat your rock candy. Pull up on the pencil to remove the rock candy from the jar. With scissors, cut the weight and the pencil from the string. You can break off little pieces of candy or eat the whole thing like a lollipop.

On the shores of Chesapeake Bay, Maryland has some of the best seafood in the country. The small town of Crisfield, Maryland, hosts one of the oldest annual seafood festivals in the United States. Each year Crisfield sponsors a crab-picking contest (picking crabmeat out of the shell), a crab-cooking contest, a crab-crawling (racing) contest, and a Crab Derby Parade. They even crown a "Miss Crustacean"!

Nickname: "Old Line State"

Capital: Annapolis

MARYLAND

PATTY-CAKE CRAB CAKES

What you need:

- 1 pound (16 ounces) canned crab meat, drained
- 4 saltine crackers, crumbled
- 1 tablespoon parsley
- ½ teaspoon Worcestershire sauce
- 3 shakes Tabasco™ sauce
- 1 egg, beaten
- ½ teaspoon Old Bay™ seasoning
- ½ teaspoon salt
- ¼ teaspoon pepper
- ¼ teaspoon paprika
- 1 cup mayonnaise

What you do:

1. Preheat oven to 350 degrees.
2. In a large bowl, combine the crab, crackers, parsley, Worcestershire sauce, Tabasco™ sauce, egg, seasonings, and 3/4 cup of the mayonnaise. Save the remaining 1/4 cup mayonnaise.

3. With your hands, form the mixture into 6 cakes. Place the cakes on a foil-covered cookie sheet.

4. Spread each crab cake with an equal portion of the reserved mayonnaise and sprinkle each one with paprika.

5. Bake for 20 minutes or until golden brown. Do not overbake!

Serves 6

Did you know that parsley "cures" bad breath? Parsley contains lots of chlorophyll that, when digested, sweetens the air in your lungs.

Native Americans lived in what is now the state of Massachusetts long before the first Europeans arrived. They taught the first colonists to plant, harvest, and prepare native foods such as corn, pumpkin, and beans the "American" way. Before long, the settlers developed their own ways of preparing these native foods.

Boston was founded in 1630 as a tightly knit village of Puritan craftsmen, farmers, and ministers. They had left England to make their homes in Massachusetts because they wanted the freedom to live according to their religious beliefs. One of the Puritans' religious beliefs was that Sunday should be a day of rest in which no work was done. This meant that meals eaten on Sunday must be prepared on Saturday. Boston Baked Beans, as they came to be known, eventually became a traditional Saturday-night supper for folks all over Massachusetts. In days gone by, homemakers would mix up their own versions of baked beans on a Saturday morning, then carry them in stoneware crocks to the neighborhood brick-oven bakery, where the beans would slow-cook all day. Today, most baked beans come out of a can.

Nickname: "Bay State"

Capital: Boston

MASSACHUSETTS

SUGAR-BAKED BEANS
What you need:
- (2) 16-ounce cans baked beans
- ½ cup ketchup
- 2 ½ tablespoons molasses
- 2 ½ tablespoons brown sugar
- 4 slices bacon or 2 hot dogs cut into ½-inch pieces

What you do:
1. Preheat oven to 350 degrees.
2. Mix together all ingredients except bacon or hot dogs.
3. Put bean mixture into a shallow, greased baking dish. Arrange slices of bacon or sliced hot dogs on top.
4. Bake, covered, about 30 minutes. Uncover and bake 30 minutes more.

Boston is nicknamed "Bean Town" for this popular bean dish.

Battle Creek, Michigan, is the home of Kellogg and Post cereal makers. More cereal and cereal products are produced here than in any city on earth! Here Doctor J. P. Kellogg, the medical superintendent of Battle Creek Hospital, invented the first flaked breakfast cereal (it was made of wheat) in 1895. Dr. Kellogg's brother, William, invented corn flakes in 1898.

Nickname: "Wolverine State"

Capital: Lansing

MICHIGAN

SNAP, CRACKLE, CRUNCH SNACK

What you need:
- ¼ cup butter or margarine
- 1 tablespoon Worcestershire sauce
- 6 drops Tabasco™ sauce (you can put more in if you like it hot!)
- 1 cup salted mixed nuts
- 1 cup pretzel sticks
- 1 cup each: Rice Krispies™, Wheat Chex™, Cheerios™
- 1 teaspoon paprika
- ¼ teaspoon onion powder
- ¼ teaspoon garlic powder

What you do:
1. Preheat oven to 250 degrees.
2. Melt the butter in a large baking pan in the oven.
3. Using an oven mitt, remove the pan from the oven in order to add the other ingredients.
4. Add the Worcestershire and Tabasco™ sauces and stir.
5. Stir in nuts and pretzels and add the cereals.
6. Add the seasonings and mix well.
7. Bake for 20–30 minutes, stirring every 10 minutes.
8. Remove the pan from the oven with an oven mitt and pour your snack into a big bowl.

You can store the party snack in a large sealable plastic bag or a sealed container.

WHY DO RICE KRISPIES™ GO "SNAP, CRACKLE, POP"?

Rice Krispies™ are made from kernels of rice. First the kernels are steamed. During this process, the kernels fill with tiny air bubbles that make them puff up. Next the puffed-up kernels are flattened. Then they're roasted till crisp. When the kernels are moistened with milk, they swell again, causing the crisp part of the kernel to break—with an energetic "snap, crackle, pop"!

In the late 1800s and early 1900s, famine in Sweden forced many Swedes to leave their homeland. Thousands headed for Minnesota, where the countryside and climate were much like Sweden's and where land was cheap and plentiful. Minnesota winters, like those in Sweden, could be bitterly cold. Rich, nourishing foods from the old country, like these Swedish meatballs, kept those Minnesota Swedes warm through many a long winter.

Nickname: "North Star State"

Capital: Saint Paul

MINNESOTA

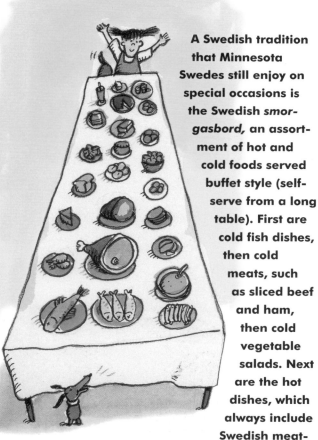

A Swedish tradition that Minnesota Swedes still enjoy on special occasions is the Swedish *smorgasbord,* an assortment of hot and cold foods served buffet style (self-serve from a long table). First are cold fish dishes, then cold meats, such as sliced beef and ham, then cold vegetable salads. Next are the hot dishes, which always include Swedish meatballs. Last are desserts—usually cheese, fresh fruit, and pastry.

MINNE MEATBALLS

What you need:

- 1 pound hamburger meat
- 1 teaspoon salt
- 10 saltine crackers, crumbled
- 2 eggs
- 1 small onion, grated
- 1 teaspoon oregano
- ½ teaspoon allspice
- 4 tablespoons milk

What you do:

1. Mix all the ingredients together in a large bowl. If the mixture falls apart, keep adding additional tablespoons of milk until the mixture stays together.

2. Using your hands, form golf-ball-sized balls with the meat mixture until you have used it up.

3. Carefully place the meatballs into a frying pan and cook on medium-low heat until browned on all sides.

You can eat the meatballs as a snack, or place them on top of cooked noodles or rice for a meal.

Ever heard the phrase "Southern hospitality"? In the southern state of Mississippi, gracious hosts and hostesses make their guests feel welcome the same way their great-grandparents did—by serving them dinner from tables laden with rich Southern dishes. One of these, Mississippi Mud Pie, named for the thick, rich, dark mud of the mighty Mississippi River, will always be a favorite!

Nickname: "Magnolia State"

Capital: Jackson

MISSISSIPPI

MISSISSIPPI MUD PIE

What you need:
- ½ pound butter, softened
- 1 ½ cups sugar
- 3 squares unsweetened chocolate, melted and cooled
- 2 teaspoons vanilla
- 1 8-ounce carton egg substitute
- (1) 9-inch prepared pie crust

Toppings: whipped cream, chocolate chips, chopped nuts, chocolate syrup

What you do:

1. In a medium-sized bowl, mash butter and sugar together with a wooden spoon and then add the chocolate and vanilla, stirring well.

2. Add eggs to the butter mixture one at a time. Beat each egg for 5 minutes with an electric mixer at medium speed. (Ask for help if you need to give your arm a rest!)

3. Pour mixture into the pie shell and refrigerate for several hours to set.

4. Top with one or all of the toppings.

Serves 6

What grows on trees, is shaped like a melon, and is full of beans? Cacao pods, used to make one of America's favorite treats—chocolate! Chocolate is made from the seeds of a tropical cacao tree. Many years ago *cacao* became know as *cocoa*, just because someone goofed up the spelling. The Indians of Central America were cultivating chocolate long before Columbus' arrival.

"**M**eet me in St. Louis, meet me at the fair!" was a line from a popular tune in 1904, when people from all over the world flocked to St. Louis, Missouri, for the World's Fair. One of the new inventions introduced at the Fair was a real hit. It was the ice cream cone.

Ice cream had already been around a long time. In 1295 Marco Polo took a recipe for a fruit ice—made with fruit juice, sugar, and water—back to Europe from Asia. Ice cream was invented three hundred years later in France, when cream was added to the recipe. But it was in St. Louis that citizens of the world first tasted ice cream atop a crisp, slightly sweet, cone-shaped wafer. Now the whole world loves an ice cream cone!

Nickname: "Show Me State"

Capital: Jefferson City

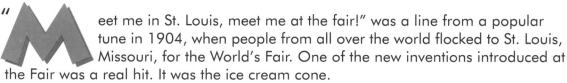

MISSOURI

SHOW-ME CREAM 'N' CONE

What you need:

- 4 egg yolks (carefully separated from white parts)
- 2 teaspoons vanilla
- 2 cups sugar
- 4 cups milk
- 1 cup water
- 1 cup heavy cream
- Hand-cranked or electric ice-cream maker
- Cones: see next recipe

What you do:

1. In a large saucepan, combine the egg yolks, vanilla, and 1 cup of the sugar, and beat with a wire whisk until the mixture is light yellow in color. Set aside.

2. In a small saucepan, heat the milk, but don't boil.

3. Gradually add the milk to the yolk mixture, beating constantly with a wooden spoon. Cook the sauce until it is very thin. It will look watery.

4. Pour mixture into a cold bowl and set aside.

5. Combine water and the remaining 1 cup of sugar in a saucepan. Stir and bring to a boil. Simmer for 10 minutes and remove from heat. Let cool.

6. If you would like to add a fruit flavor, put a handful of the fruit of your choice into a food processor or blender and blend thoroughly. You can do the same with chocolate (1/2 cup, or to taste) if you would like chocolate ice cream.

7. Combine the yolk and sugar mixtures together and add fruit mixture if desired.

8. Whip the cream (heavy cream needs to be beaten with an electric mixer for several minutes to thicken).

9. Pour the cream into the yolk and sugar mixture and gently stir together. There will be a container in the electric or hand-cranked ice-cream maker that you will need to pour your mixture into. Put the container into the freezer and freeze according to directions.

10. Scoop onto a cone. (See next recipe.)

HOMEMADE CONES

What you need:

- 3 tablespoons butter, at room temperature
- 1 cup brown sugar
- 2 tablespoons honey
- 1 egg
- 2 tablespoons flour
- ¼ teaspoon salt

What you do:

1. Preheat oven to 350 degrees.

2. Put all the ingredients in a blender and blend on high until the batter is smooth. The batter should drop from a spoon easily, so if it seems too thick, add a little water and blend again.

3. Drop a tablespoon of batter onto a well-greased cookie sheet. Each cookie should be about 7 inches apart.

4. Bake the cookies for 4–5 minutes. Remove them from the oven. Let them cool only a second or two before removing them from the cookie sheet with a spatula onto a rack or piece of foil on the counter.

5. Loosely curl each cookie around the handle of a wooden spoon while it is still warm. Pinch the bottom and the open side together to make a cone. Make sure the top is wider than the rest of the cone.

6. When the cones have hardened, fill them with your favorite ice cream!

Makes about 6 large or 8 small cones

A Dip Tip: Placing a marshmallow in the bottom of an ice cream cone keeps melting ice cream from leaking.

That'll be two bits, Jed.

Beef jerky, a popular snack sold at convenience stores all over America, has been around for thousands of years. The name *jerky* came from the word *charqui,* from the language of the Quechua Indians of South America. When white people first began settling the West into parts of what is now Montana, they had no way to refrigerate meat. They learned to preserve it the way the Indians did—by cutting it into long, thick strips and drying it.

Cowboys and prospectors carried it in saddlebags for a quick meal while they were on the move. Although jerky was originally dried by smoking it over an open fire, it can now be made in an oven with flavored spices to provide the smoky, open-fire flavor.

Nickname: "Big Sky Country"

Capital: Helena

MONTANA

MOUNTAIN MAN JERKY

What you need:

- 1 ½ pounds lean meat, such as rump roast or top sirloin roast. Ask your butcher to slice it thin for jerky and trim off all fat and gristle.
- 3/4 cup water
- 1 teaspoon garlic powder
- 1 teaspoon chili powder
- 1/2 teaspoon hickory sauce or teriyaki sauce

What you do:

1. In a large bowl, combine all the ingredients except the meat.

2. Add the meat to the mixture and let it sit for about 3 ½ hours. This is called *marinating*. If you want to marinate the meat overnight, cover the bowl and put it in the refrigerator.

3. Preheat oven to 200 degrees.

4. Carefully lay the strips of meat directly on an oven rack. Make sure that the rack is at least 2 inches above a pan that can catch the drippings. (Another way to cook the jerky is to push a toothpick through one end of each of the strips. Then hang them from the oven rack over a pan that will catch the drippings.)

6. Bake for 4–6 hours, or until the strips are dry enough to crack but don't break when you bend them.

Store in a tightly sealed container or sealable plastic bag. The jerky will keep for a long time.

45

NEBRASKA

Nebraska means cattle and cattle means beef! So much cattle and beef, in fact, that Nebraska is our nation's leading producer of beef cattle and is the meatpacking capital of the world. Ninety-five percent of Nebraska's land is in farms, a percentage higher than any other state. Nebraska's largest farms are cattle ranches, some covering more than 100,000 acres. Thousands upon thousands of cattle graze the rich, native range grasses; many more thousands are shipped to the corn-growing farms of Nebraska to be fattened up on corn before being sent to market.

Nebraskans chow down on lots of their own corn-fed beef and claim their burgers are the best! Here's the story of hamburgers:

The Tartars, roving horsemen who lived in Asia, were tough guys who ate raw meat. But all that chewing got old, and eventually the Tartars came up with a way to tenderize their meat—by tucking it under their saddles while they rode all over the great grasslands. By dinnertime, the meat had been bumped and pounded to a tender pulp. All a Tartar had to do was remove his saddle, season his meat, and voilá! Tender, tasty steak Tartar.

In the mid-1800s, a trader from Hamburg, Germany, took the Tartar's way of tenderizing meat back to Germany, where it became known as Hamburg steak. German settlers brought Hamburg steak to the United States. In 1904, at the World's Fair in St. Louis, Missouri, hamburger patties were broiled, served on buns, and, for the first time, called "hamburgers."

I sure could use some fries and a drink with this.

> **Americans eat more than 40 billion hamburgers a year.**

> **Steak tartare—raw, seasoned, ground beef—is still served in some fancy restaurants!**

CORNHUSKER BURGERS

What you need:

- 1 ½ pounds ground hamburger meat
- 4 tablespoons barbecue sauce
- 6 American cheese slices
- Cookie cutter (optional)
- 6 hamburger buns
- Toppings (ketchup, mustard, mayonnaise, lettuce, tomato, pickles)

What you do:

1. Mix hamburger with barbecue sauce.
2. Form the ground beef into 6 patties and place them in a large frying pan.
3. Cook on medium heat for about 4 minutes, then carefully turn them over with a spatula.
4. When the meat is almost done (about 3 minutes more), place a slice of cheese on each patty. Cover the pan and cook a minute longer so the cheese melts. You can first cut the cheese with a cookie cutter and put the shaped cheese on top of the meat.

> **The largest hamburger on record weighed 5,520 pounds and was 21 feet in diameter.**

5. Put the hamburger patties on top of the bun bottoms and add any toppings before putting the top bun on.

Serve with potato chips or carrot sticks.

Serves 6

I sure could use some fries and a drink with this.

47

In the 1870s, hundreds of Basque sheepherders from the Pyrenees Mountains of northeastern Spain and southwestern France migrated to Nevada. These men spent many long, lonely hours tending flocks of sheep in Nevada's high mountains, hoping to make enough money to provide a better life for the families and friends they'd left behind. Whenever they had a chance, they would head to the nearest town with a Basque hotel to rest, talk, hear the latest news from back home, and eat generous, home-cooked, family-style Basque meals. Such meals usually included beef and lamb steaks, chorizo (a spicy Basque sausage), soup, beans, fried potatoes, spaghetti, bread, and flan, a delicious baked caramel custard, for dessert.

Nickname: "Silver State"

Capital: Carson City

NEVADA

Nevada's fabled Comstock Lode, an incredibly rich gold and silver deposit, inspired a wild and woolly bonanza. Nevada is still the largest producer of gold in the United States.

GOLD NUGGET FLAN

What you need:

- ½ cup granulated sugar
- (1) 14-ounce can sweetened condensed milk
- 1 cup milk
- 3 large eggs
- 3 large egg yolks (carefully separated from white parts)
- ½ teaspoon almond extract
- 1 teaspoon vanilla
- 1 cup butterscotch pieces

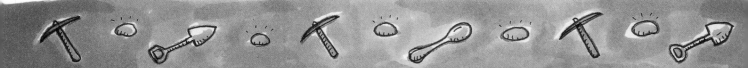

What you do:

1. Preheat oven to 325 degrees.

2. In a small saucepan, melt sugar over medium heat, stirring frequently until sugar is a dark, caramel-colored liquid.

3. Remove from heat and pour into a 4-cup ring mold. Let cool so that the caramel hardens.

4. Put remaining ingredients (except butterscotch pieces) into an electric blender and mix well.

5. Pour this mixture into the mold on top of the hardened caramel. Put the mold in a larger pan filled with water ½-inch deep.

6. Bake 1 hour.

7. With oven mitts, carefully take the pans out of the oven and set on counter to cool. Take the mold pan out of the pan with water and put it into the refrigerator to chill.

8. To serve, cover the top of the mold pan with a plate and turn upside-down. Remove the mold. The caramel sauce will drizzle down over the set custard. Sprinkle with butterscotch pieces.

Basque restaurants in Nevada still serve meals family-style, with customers seated side by side at long tables. This arrangement makes it easy for strangers to become friends!

Nevada means *snowy* in Spanish. Spanish explorers named the area for the snowcapped mountains in west-central Nevada.

Native, all-American blueberries have covered gravelly hillsides and mountaintops all over the state of New Hampshire for as long as anyone can remember. A blueberry plant sends out underground stems called *rhizomes*. As rhizomes grow out all around the plant, they send up new shoots. The new shoots, which develop their own roots, grow to be four to eighteen inches tall. Gradually a very large, interconnected mass of roots, shoots, and underground rhizomes develops, covering an area up to 250 square feet. This spreading plant complex is called a *clone*.

Wild berries are about the size of a pea. Cultivated berries can grow to be almost an inch in diameter. Many of New Hampshire's berries are turned into jams, jellies, sauces, pies, juices, and syrups.

Nickname: "Granite State"

Capital: Concord

NEW HAMPSHIRE

TRUE BLUE SOUP

What you need:
- 2 cups fresh or frozen blueberries
- ¾ cup lemon juice
- 1 ¼ cups cranberry juice
- ½ cup sugar
- 2 cups whipped cream

Bears love blueberries. Folks in New Hampshire are accustomed to seeing chubby black bears scooping up all the berries within arm's reach and tossing them into their mouths. Bears gorge on berries in preparation for long, cold New Hampshire winters.

What you do:

1. Put blueberries in a blender and puree until smooth.

2. In a medium saucepan, combine the blueberries, lemon juice, cranberry juice, and sugar. Stir until mixed together.

3. Simmer on low heat, covered, for 10 minutes.

4. Turn heat off and let cool (about 20 minutes).

5. Gently stir in the whipped cream. Put pan in the refrigerator and chill for 3 hours.

6. Pour the soup into small bowls and enjoy with fresh blueberries on the side.

Serves 4

New Jersey is one of our country's top producers of the all-American cranberry, one of only a handful of major fruits that are native to North America. Cranberries are grown in sandy bogs (wet, spongy ground) under conditions that wouldn't support other crops: acid soil, few nutrients, and low temperatures. When the cranberries are ready for harvest, the bogs are flooded and the floating berries are scooped from the water. The average acre of cranberry bog is surrounded by 4–10 acres of wetlands and woodlands that offer refuge to a rich variety of wildlife.

Nickname: "Garden State"

Capital: Trenton

NEW JERSEY

One . . .

IT'S THE BERRIES!
What you need:
- 1 cup sour cream
- 1 teaspoon vanilla
- 1 teaspoon salt
- 1 ½ cups brown sugar
- ⅔ cup vegetable oil
- 1 egg
- 2 ½ cups flour
- 1 ½ cups cranberries
- ½ cup pecans, chopped
- 2 tablespoons sugar
- Butter for topping

It takes 4,400 cranberries to make one gallon of juice!

Long before Europeans arrived, Native Americans mixed cranberries with deer meat and melted fat to make *pemmican,* a high-energy, dried food that would keep for a long time. Medicine men concocted cranberry poultices to pull poison from arrow wounds. Squaws dyed their rugs and blankets with the berries' red juice.

What you do:
1. Preheat oven to 325 degrees.
2. In a small bowl, stir together sour cream, vanilla, and salt with a spoon.
3. In another small bowl, combine brown sugar, oil, and egg with an electric mixer.
4. Pour both mixtures into a large mixing bowl and mix together.
5. Gradually add the flour to the mixture. Fold in cranberries and pecans without stirring too thoroughly.
6. Pour batter into cups of a greased muffin pan. Sprinkle tops with sugar and place a dab of butter on each.
7. Bake for 30 minutes.

Makes 12–15 muffins

From 1540–42, Spanish explorers traveled throughout what is now New Mexico searching for the legendary Seven Cities of Gold, long-lost cities that were said to be built of silver and gold and filled with fabulous treasures. The explorers, hoping this new land would make them as rich as Mexico had, called it *un nuevo Mexico*—a new Mexico.

Although the Seven Cities were never found (most people now think the stories about them were just made up), New Mexico is rich indeed—in character. New Mexico is unlike any other state: its history includes ancient Indian civilizations and 250 years of Spanish rule and association with Mexico. Its people are a distinctive mixture of Native Americans, Hispanics, and Anglos, many of whom speak Spanish or an Indian language in addition to English. You can taste that distinctive mixture in the food of New Mexico as well.

NEW MEXICO

Nickname: "Land of Enchantment"

Capital: Santa Fe

BUENOS DIAS (GOOD DAY) TORTILLAS

What you need:
- (1) 14 ½-ounce can Mexican-style stewed tomatoes, diced
- (5) 6-inch corn tortillas
- 1 can refried beans
- 1 cup grated Monterey Jack cheese
- 1 cup grated cheddar cheese
- ½ cup black olives, pitted and sliced

What you do:
1. Preheat oven to 450 degrees.
2. In a round, 9-inch baking dish, spread 1/4 cup of the diced tomatoes in the bottom of the dish. Place a tortilla on top, spread a layer of beans on it, and sprinkle with ⅓ cup of each cheese and a few olive slices. Repeat the layering until you use up all of your ingredients.
3. Put any extra cheese you have on the top layer.
4. Bake about 10–12 minutes or until the cheese is melted.
5. Cut into wedges and serve (serves 4).

New Mexico's state vegetables are chile peppers and frijoles (pinto beans).

New York, New York, the largest city in the United States, is a city of migrants and immigrants, a place where newspapers are published in at least twenty-four different languages! Millions of immigrants have come to America by way of New York, and many of them have stayed to make New York their home. In the early part of this century, more than half the city's working population was foreign-born.

Many of the immigrants were Jewish people; so many, in fact, that New York City now has the largest Jewish population of any city in the world. Even after years of living in New York, many of them continue to speak Yiddish (the language of Jewish people from Europe and Russia) and prepare their food in traditional Jewish ways. One of the best-known Jewish foods is the bagel, a doughnut-shaped yeast bread, often eaten with cream cheese.

Nickname: "Empire State"

Capital: Albany

NEW YORK

DELISH DELI DUO

What you need:
- (2) 3-ounce packages cream cheese
- ¼ cup vanilla yogurt
- 1 ½ teaspoons sugar
- 3 tablespoons raspberry preserves
- 6 bagels, any flavor, presliced

New York is famous for its delicatessens, food shops with a variety of specially prepared, ready-to-eat, cooked meats, fish, cheeses, salads, and breads. Bagels are favorite deli fare.

What you do:

1. Combine cream cheese, yogurt, and sugar in a food processor, or mix with an electric mixer until smooth.

2. Alternately spoon cream cheese mixture and raspberry preserves into a small serving bowl. Gently stir in a circular motion to form swirls without mixing the two completely together.

3. Spread on top of sliced bagels.

Makes 1 cup of topping

Home gardens provided many of the basic foods for Southern meals in the past. A typical North Carolina garden in the 1800s would certainly have included sweet potatoes. (Today North Carolina produces more sweet potatoes than any other state!) Because the area's long growing season meant lots of the same vegetables over and over, Southerners came up with many different ways to prepare these foods. Sweet potatoes, for example, were baked in casseroles, pies, puddings, and even breads. These are still favorite dishes.

Nickname: "Tarheel State"

Capital: Raleigh

NORTH CAROLINA

SWEETIE PIE POTATOES
What you need:
- 3 sweet potatoes, washed and pricked with a fork
- 1 tablespoon butter
- ¼ cup cream, heated
- ¼ teaspoon salt
- 2 tablespoons brown sugar
- 1 teaspoon nutmeg
- 1 small bag miniature marshmallows

Y'all are just so sweet!

What you do:
1. Preheat oven to 425 degrees.
2. Cut a slice off one end of each potato, place each directly on oven rack, and bake for 1 hour. With oven mitts, take potatoes out and turn oven down to 375 degrees.
3. Still using oven mitts, hold onto the hot potatoes, cut them lengthwise into halves, and scrape out the pulp with a spoon. (Careful—they're hot!)
4. Put potato pulp in a bowl and add all ingredients, except marshmallows.
5. Use a fork and beat mixture until it's very fluffy.
6. Fill the potato shells with potato mixture and arrange marshmallows on top.
7. Put filled shells on a cookie sheet and bake until the marshmallows are golden brown (approximately 5 minutes).

Serves 6

54

Wheat is the world's largest crop. Every minute of every day, all year long, someone, somewhere, is planting wheat while someone else is harvesting it. North Dakota, one of the United States' top producers of wheat, is famous for its hardy *durum,* the kind of wheat used to make the best pasta. Chances are, when you eat spaghetti or macaroni and cheese, you're eating North Dakota-grown durum wheat.

Pasta is the Italian word for dough.

NORTH DAKOTA

Nickname: "Sioux State"

Capital: Bismarck

LITTLE MAC & BIG CHEESE

What you need:

- 2 cups shell or elbow macaroni (made with 100% durum wheat semolina)
- 1 ½ quarts salted water
- 2 cups cheddar cheese, shredded
- 3 eggs, well beaten with 2 tablespoons milk
- Salt and pepper to taste
- ⅓ cup bread crumbs

Pasta dishes have been a specialty of Italy since the 1200s; now they're popular all over the world. Pasta comes in more than 100 shapes and sizes.

What you do:

1. Preheat oven to 325 degrees.

2. Bring water to boil, then add macaroni. Boil, uncovered, for 10–12 minutes, stirring occasionally. Drain well.

3. Pour macaroni into a medium-sized bowl. Add cheese, egg mixture, and salt and pepper. Mix well.

4. Pour mixture into greased casserole dish. Cover with foil.

5. Bake for 20 minutes or until eggs are firm.

6. With pot holders, take the dish from the oven. Carefully uncover.

7. Sprinkle top with bread crumbs. Return to oven. Broil, uncovered, until crust is formed (just a minute or two).

Serves 4

Ohio is a true "melting pot" state, with citizens of German, Irish, Russian, English, Polish, Czechoslovakian, Hungarian, and every European background. During the early 1800s, most of Ohio's settlers came from eastern states. But after 1830, large numbers of European immigrants began traveling directly to Ohio, hoping to find work in the factories of Ohio's large industrial cities.

Markets such as the famous West Side Market in Cleveland sell all kinds of special meats and cheeses prepared in the European ways that Ohio's newcomers were accustomed to. Various type of sausages (cured beef, veal, or pork, usually stuffed into a casing) are particularly popular.

OHIO

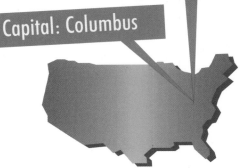

Nickname: "Buckeye State"

Capital: Columbus

DOGS IN A BLANKET
What you need:
- 4 cups water
- 4 frankfurters
- 4 flour tortillas
- 1 tomato, sliced
- ¾ cup cheddar cheese, grated
- 4 pieces cooked bacon
- Ketchup, mustard, relish, and other toppings of your choice (for a German taste, spoon a little sauerkraut or spicy mustard on your frankfurter)

What you do:
1. Boil the water in a medium saucepan. Carefully add the frankfurters and cook for about 5 minutes. Using tongs, remove them from the water and place onto a paper towel.

2. Take one tortilla and spread any or all of the condiments on it. Slice the frankfurter lengthwise (careful—it's hot!) and place the two pieces on one side of the tortilla.

3. On top of the frankfurter, add a slice of tomato and enough cheese to cover the hot dog. With your hands, crumble a piece of bacon on top of the cheese. Add any other desired toppings.

4. Fold both sides of the tortilla towards the middle and then roll the tortilla over the hot dog to form a burrito. Now repeat steps 2–4 for the remaining three frankfurters. Serve with chips or fries.

Makes 4 frankfurter burritos

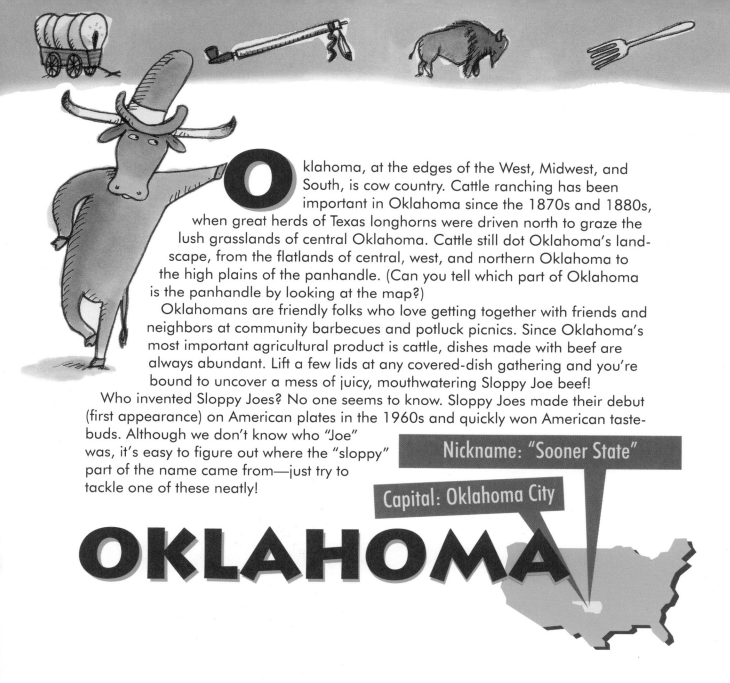

Oklahoma, at the edges of the West, Midwest, and South, is cow country. Cattle ranching has been important in Oklahoma since the 1870s and 1880s, when great herds of Texas longhorns were driven north to graze the lush grasslands of central Oklahoma. Cattle still dot Oklahoma's landscape, from the flatlands of central, west, and northern Oklahoma to the high plains of the panhandle. (Can you tell which part of Oklahoma is the panhandle by looking at the map?)

Oklahomans are friendly folks who love getting together with friends and neighbors at community barbecues and potluck picnics. Since Oklahoma's most important agricultural product is cattle, dishes made with beef are always abundant. Lift a few lids at any covered-dish gathering and you're bound to uncover a mess of juicy, mouthwatering Sloppy Joe beef!

Who invented Sloppy Joes? No one seems to know. Sloppy Joes made their debut (first appearance) on American plates in the 1960s and quickly won American taste-buds. Although we don't know who "Joe" was, it's easy to figure out where the "sloppy" part of the name came from—just try to tackle one of these neatly!

Nickname: "Sooner State"

Capital: Oklahoma City

OKLAHOMA

SOONER SLOPPIES

What you need:

- 1 pound lean ground beef
- 1 cup chopped onion
- 2 cloves garlic, minced (chopped into tiny pieces)
- ¼ teaspoon each salt and pepper
- (1) 15-ounce can tomato sauce
- ½ cup water (you may need to add a little more if the mixture is too thick)
- ½ cup ketchup
- 1 teaspoon Worcestershire sauce
- 1 tablespoon cider vinegar
- 4 hamburger buns, sliced and warmed

What you do:

1. In a large frying pan over medium-high heat, cook the ground beef. Using a wooden spoon, break up the meat into small pieces. Add the onion, garlic, salt, and pepper. Cook until the meat is browned, about 10 minutes. Carefully remove any grease from the pan with a spoon.

2. Add the tomato sauce and water to the meat mixture. Turn the heat to low and simmer, uncovered, for about 10 minutes, stirring occasionally.

3. Add the ketchup, Worcestershire sauce, and vinegar. Stir constantly, cooking until the mixture is thick but not hard. If it is too thick, you can add a little more water; if it's too thin, just cook it a little longer.

4. Place the bottom half of a bun on a plate and spoon the Sloppy Joe mixture onto the bun. Cover with the top half of the bun. You can put as much of the mixture on your bun as you like. The more you pile on, the sloppier it will be! (You can always eat it with a knife and fork, but it's more fun to pick it up and eat it.)

Serves 4

Hey, this is OK!

Thanks to the rich soil of Oregon's Willamette Valley—some of the best agricultural land in the world—Oregon produces a staggering 35,000 tons of sweet cherries each year. An average of 18,700 tons (that's more than 37 MILLION pounds!) of Oregon cherries are "brined" and made into maraschinos, those shiny, red, ice-cream-sundae toppers.

It's important to eat some fresh fruit every day, because fruit is chock-full of vitamins, minerals, and fiber.

Nickname: "Beaver State"

Capital: Salem

OREGON

VERY CHERRY & CREAM

What you need:
- ½ cup heavy cream
- 1 tablespoon honey
- ¼ teaspoon vanilla
- 1 cup cherries, washed, pitted, and stems removed

What you do:

1. In a small bowl, mix cream, honey, and vanilla.

2. Put cherries in a small dessert dish.

3. Pour the cream mixture over the cherries and enjoy!

Examine your tongue. See all those bumps? No, they're not taste buds. They're the *papillae*, and there are hundreds of them. Your taste buds, thousands of them, are on the papillae. Though they're too small for you to see, they determine whether you like cherries (most people do) or caviar (very iffy).

Your taste buds recognize only four tastes: salty, sweet, sour, and bitter. Try this experiment: Place a spot of honey or sugar in different places on your tongue. Does it taste different, depending on where it is? Try the same thing with lemon juice, vinegar, and salt. Now taste a variety of foods while wearing a blindfold and holding your nose. Try to guess what food each taste goes with. Which are easiest to guess, even when you can't see or smell them? See how important your sense of smell is to your sense of taste?

You have more tastebuds than your mom and dad have. You have fewer than your younger brother or sister. People lose tastebuds as they grow older.

PENNSYLVANIA

Nickname: "Keystone State"

Capital: Harrisburg

By the early 1700s, the colony of Pennsylvania was home to people of many different religions and nationalities. The largest group to settle in Pennsylvania were German immigrants, who came to the New World in search of religious freedom. Despite the fact that they weren't from the Netherlands, they became known as the "Dutch." Here's why: Their non-German neighbors called them *Pennsylvania Deutsch*, because *Deutsch* means *German* in the German language. Many thousands of descendants of the Pennsylvania Dutch colonists still live in Pennsylvania. One of their favorite desserts, now as in the time of their great-great-grandfathers, is funnel cake. You might have eaten funnel cake at a state fair. Now you can make your own!

Baking powder is used in recipes for baked goods that don't call for yeast, such as biscuits, muffins, waffles, cookies, and cakes.

60

DUTCH-TREAT FUNNEL CAKES

(Note: Ask your adult assistant for help with this recipe.)

What you need:
- 1 egg
- 1 ¼ cups flour
- 2 tablespoons sugar
- 1 teaspoon baking powder
- ¼ teaspoon salt
- ⅔ cup milk
- ¼ cup powdered sugar
- 2 cups oil for frying
- Funnel

What you do:

1. In a large bowl, beat egg on low speed with an electric mixer. Add the dry ingredients except for powdered sugar and mix together with a wooden spoon.

2. Add the milk to the mixture gradually, and beat it with an electric mixer on low speed until it looks smooth and creamy.

3. In a medium-sized frying pan, heat the oil.

4. Using a funnel, pour the batter through the funnel and into the oil and swirl the batter with a wooden spoon in a circular motion. The more batter you pour into the funnel, the bigger the cake. You can make big and small cakes if you wish.

5. Cook for about 2 minutes, then turn funnel cake over with a spatula and cook the other side for 2 minutes.

6. Set each funnel cake on a paper towel to eliminate any extra oil.

7. Put the funnel cakes onto a plate and sprinkle a little powdered sugar on each one.

What a gas!

MIX a teaspoon of baking powder in a cup of warm water. See how the water bubbles? Baking powder contains a base (baking soda) and an acid. Bases and acids are chemical compounds that react together. As soon as baking powder is added to a liquid (batter, for instance) the base and acid react, producing carbon-dioxide bubbles. Carbon-dioxide bubbles puff up batter so that it rises while baking.

Which came first, the chicken or the egg? The chicken—to America, at least! Christopher Columbus brought a bunch of them in 1493 on his second voyage to the New World.

Until the mid-1800s, most Americans lived in the country and had chickens of their own to supply their eggs. But as more and more Americans moved to cities, some farmers began to specialize in chickens, producing thousands of eggs each week to sell to the growing numbers of city folks.

Two Rhode Island chicken farmers, Isaac Wilbour and William Tripp, began crossbreeding different kinds of chickens until they came up with a new kind of chicken that required little care and could lay more and bigger eggs. Because these new chickens had red feathers, Wilbour named them Rhode Island Reds.

Wilbour began to advertise his Reds in poultry journals. As the chickens' reputation spread, farmers all over Rhode Island, then all across America, began to raise Reds. Now people all over the world—from remote, icy burgs to tropical, thatched-roof villages—keep Rhode Island Reds for their eggs.

Nickname: "Little Rhody"

Capital: Providence

RHODE ISLAND

Eggs are an important part of most Americans' diets. The yolk and white contain fat (which gives us energy), protein (which strengthens our bodies), and vitamins and minerals (which keep us healthy). Even if you don't eat eggs for breakfast, you probably get your share. Eggs are an ingredient in many prepared foods—cake and ice cream, for instance.

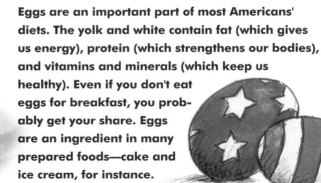

LITTLE RHODY FRIED EGG-IN-A-HOLE

What you need:
- 1 slice of bread
- 1 teaspoon butter or margarine
- 1 small round glass or small cookie cutter, any shape
- 1 egg

What you do:

1. Butter both sides of bread.

2. Press the glass or cookie cutter into the middle of the bread. Remove the shape from the bread and set aside.

3. Put the piece of bread (minus the middle) into a small frying pan on medium heat. Crack the egg and make sure that the egg goes in the hole.

4. Cook the egg until the yolk is hard. Carefully slide a spatula under both the bread and the egg and flip it to brown the other side.

5. Just before the egg is done, add the middle piece of bread to the pan and brown on both sides. This becomes a little piece of toast to go with your egg-in-a-hole!

HOW FRESH IS THAT EGG?

Stir a teaspoon of salt into a glass of water. Ease a whole, uncracked egg into the water with a spoon. If the egg floats to the top of the water, it's old. Don't eat it! As an egg ages, the white evaporates, leaving just air. The more air an egg contains, the easier it is for the egg to float.

The yolk of a just-cracked egg will be firm and rounded, and the white will be thick. The yolk of an old egg will be flat and thin, and the white will be watery.

The Rhode Island Red is Rhode Island's official state bird.

63

Grits have been called the first truly American food. Here's why: One day in the spring of 1607, a band of English settlers finally set foot on land at Jamestown, in what is now the southern part of the state of Virginia, after months at sea. They were welcomed by friendly Indians who offered bowls of a hot porridge made of large corn grains they called *rockahominie*.

The settlers "anglicized" (that is, changed to a word that sounded more like English) the name to *hominy*. Then they found a way to dry and bleach the corn, remove the hull and germ, and grind the large corn grains into smaller particles, called grits. Grits soon became a favorite food in what are now the Southern states.

SOUTH CAROLINA

Nickname: "Palmetto State"

Capital: Columbia

GO GRITS! Every April, South Carolina hosts the World Grits Festival, where events include rolling-in-the-grits, grits-grinding, corn-shelling, and grits-eating contests!

GOOD-FOR-THE-SOUL GRITS

What you need:
- 1 cup uncooked grits
- 1 egg, beaten
- ½ cup butter
- 2 cups cheddar cheese, grated
- ½ teaspoon salt
- Pinch of pepper
- 1 tablespoon oil or butter
- 2 tablespoons parmesan cheese, grated

What you do:
1. Preheat oven to 350 degrees.
2. In a medium saucepan, cook the grits by following the basic cooking directions on the box.
3. Once you have cooked your grits, mix the egg and butter into the grits.
4. Stir in the cheddar cheese and the seasonings and mix well.
5. Pour the tablespoon of oil or butter in a 2-quart baking dish and spread it around to coat the pan evenly. You can use your hands or a paper towel.
6. Pour the grits mixture into the baking dish and sprinkle the top with the parmesan cheese.
7. Bake for 30 minutes or until the top is golden brown.

You can find grits, dried and in a box, in the cereal section of the grocery store.

SOUTH DAKOTA

Nickname: "Coyote State"

Capital: Pierre

South Dakota is famous for the Black Hills, some of the oldest mountains in the world. Wyatt Earp, Wild Bill Hickok, and Calamity Jane all spent time in the Black Hills boomtown of Deadwood, one of the most rootin', tootin', shootin' towns of the old West.

Scientists say the Black Hills were formed ages ago when a giant dome of rock pushed itself out of the earth, shoving aside everything blocking its path. The winds, rains, and ice of the ages then carved the dome into rugged peaks and valleys. But many South Dakotans give Paul Bunyan credit!

Paul Bunyan was a legendary giant lumberjack who traveled all across what is now the northwestern United States. Paul's voice was like a clap of thunder. By swinging his ax around in a circle, he could cut down all the trees withing reach. His enormous blue ox, Babe, was his helper. Babe once put out a forest fire by swallowing a fog and breathing inland!

According to South Dakota legend, the Black Hills were formed when Babe swallowed a red-hot stove and galloped, bellowing, across the prairies of South Dakota before finally dying of exhaustion and indigestion. Paul followed and sadly began to build up a great pile of earth and rocks to bury his beloved ox. The burial mound became the Black Hills. Paul cried as he worked, and his tears ran together and formed the Missouri River.

A man as large and hardworking as Paul had a huge appetitie. The griddle that cooked the flapjacks he ate every morning was so big it had to be greased by a trio of boys skating across it with slabs of bacon strapped to their feet. The boys had to finish the job and get out of the way quickly to avoid being drowned in a tidal wave of flapjack batter!

South Dakotans like their flapjacks the way Paul liked his—firm, thick, and hearty.

Firm, thick cakes like these are known as flapjacks or griddle cakes rather than pancakes.

FLAPPIN' JACKS

What you need:

- 2 cups flour
- 1 tablespoon baking powder
- 1 teaspoon salt
- 2 tablespoons sugar
- 2 eggs, well beaten
- 2 cups milk
- 5 tablespoons butter, melted

What you do:

1. In a large bowl, combine the first 4 ingredients with a spoon.

2. In a medium-sized bowl, mix the eggs, milk, and melted butter with a spoon.

3. Add the egg mixture to the dry mixture and stir quickly but not too much. (If you overstir, your flapjacks will be tough.)

4. Heat a griddle or frying pan on medium-high heat and spray with non-stick cooking spray. Using a ladle, spoon the batter onto the hot surface. Cook until the batter starts to bubble, then, with a spatula, carefully flip over and brown the other side.

5. Stack your flapjacks on a plate and

Flapjacks may be the oldest prepared food. The first flapjack batter was a mixture of ground grain and water spread on a hot stone next to an open fire.

cover with a piece of foil until you have used up all your batter. (This will keep them warm.)

6. Distribute the flapjacks on plates and serve with syrup and butter.

Makes 16 flapjacks

The southern state of Tennessee is famous for Civil War battlefields (after Virginia, Tennessee was the chief battleground of the Civil War) and delicious Southern cooking. The dinner table has always been a center of culture and tradition in Southern states such as Tennessee. Fried chicken, turkey, and ham are typical Southern main dishes. Popular side dishes include mashed potatoes, fried or boiled okra, turnip greens, and black-eyed peas. Dumplings, cornbread, corn fritters, buttermilk biscuits, hush puppies (deep-fried cornmeal balls), and a delicious, soft, custard-like concoction called spoonbread are often served instead of ordinary bread.

And for dessert? Tennessee folks love Southern pecan pie! Pecans are native only to the southern United States and grew only in the South (mostly on wild trees) until about 1900. Now there are orchards in Arizona, California, and Oregon, but—according to Southerners—the best pecans still come from the South.

Nickname: "Volunteer State"

Capital: Nashville

TENNESSEE

SUPER SOUTHERN PECAN PIE

What you need:
- 3 tablespoons butter
- 1 cup brown sugar
- 1 cup light corn syrup
- 1 teaspoon vanilla
- 3 eggs, beaten lightly
- 1 ½ cups chopped pecans
- 3 ounces bittersweet chocolate pieces, chopped
- (1) 9-inch prepared pie crust

What you do:
1. Preheat oven to 375 degrees.
2. In a saucepan, combine butter, sugar, corn syrup, and vanilla. Bring to a simmer, stirring constantly until sugar is melted. Set aside to cool.
3. Stir the beaten eggs into the sauce, and then stir in the pecans.
4. Place the chocolate pieces on the bottom of the pie crust.
5. Pour the mixture into the pie shell and bake for 30 minutes.
6. Let the pie cool, then cut into wedges and serve.

Ever wonder why butter turns darker after you place it in a butter dish in the refrigerator? Because you removed the wrapper it came in and exposed it to the air. This is called *oxidation*. It's the same thing that happens to apples and bananas after you remove their wrappers (peels).

TEXAS

Six flags have flown over Texas: the Spanish, French, Mexican, Republic of Texas, Confederate, and the Stars and Stripes of the United States. Although all have greatly influenced the food of Texas, the state is particularly famous for its Tex-Mex fare (Mexican food with American touches) and its chili (or chilli, or chile—all are acceptable spellings in Texas).

Chili is, in fact, the state dish and chili cook-offs, or contests—held in restaurants, churches, schools, shopping centers, city parks, county fairs, and just about anywhere else—are a strong Texas tradition.

Old-timers insist that "real" Texas chili has no beans and no tomatoes, but almost anything goes nowadays (cook-off entries have included turkey, olives, and anchovies). The most famous of the cook-offs, the annual International Chili Cook-off, takes place in Terlingua, Texas, on the first weekend in November.

LONE STAR CHILI & TEX-MEX CRACKERS

LONE STAR CHILI

What you need:

- 1 tablespoon vegetable oil
- 1 ½ pounds chili meat or ground beef
- 1 medium onion, chopped
- (1) 28-ounce can crushed tomatoes
- 3 cups water
- 1 tablespoon ground cumin
- 3 teaspoons chili powder
  (less if you like it less spicy)
- 1 teaspoon salt
- 1 teaspoon pepper
- ½ teaspoon red pepper (optional)
- 2 teaspoons sugar
- 1 can pinto beans, drained
- 1 can kidney beans, drained
- Cheddar cheese (optional)

What you do:

1. In a large saucepan, heat the oil over medium-high heat. Add the meat to the pan and cook, breaking it up, until meat is browned, about 10 minutes.

2. Add the onion to the pan and cook until the onion is clear and tender.

3. Add the tomatoes, water, cumin, chili powder, salt, pepper, red pepper, sugar, and beans to the pan.

4. Bring to a boil. Reduce heat to low, cover, and simmer for 45 minutes.

5. Divide the chili into small bowls and serve with tortillas or crackers. Shredded cheddar cheese can also be sprinkled on top of the chili.

TEX-MEX CRACKERS

What you need:

- (2) 12-ounce packages oyster crackers
- 1 package prepared dry taco seasoning
- ½ teaspoon chili powder
- ½ teaspoon garlic powder
- ¼ teaspoon oregano
- ¼ teaspoon cumin
- ¾ cup vegetable oil

What you do:

1. Put all the ingredients into a large sealable plastic bag.

2. Seal the bag tightly, and then shake the bag well to mix the ingredients together.

3. Put in small bowls and serve with your chili.

Hot, spicy food such as chili is often popular in hot climates—which is handy, since hot spices make food last longer without spoiling.

Hot spices also make the person eating them sweat. When sweat evaporates, the body is cooled off!

Utah, the "Beehive State," is a place where residents like to stay busy as bees. The state insect is the honeybee.

About honey: Flowers produce a sweet juice called nectar. Honeybees drink the nectar, then store it in their "honey stomachs," where it mixes with enzymes (special chemicals) from the bee's body. When a bee's honey stomach is full, it flies back to its hive and unloads the juice from its honey stomach into the cells (compartments) of the honeycomb.

The bee then seals each cell with wax. As water from the nectar evaporates from each cell, the nectar changes to honey.

Beekeepers remove the wooden frames that contain the honeycombs from man-made hives. The wooden frames are placed in a machine called a honey extractor. It cuts the wax seals off the cells, then spins the frames around until all the honey drains from the honeycomb. The honey is then poured into clean containers and sealed. The frames are put back into the beehives so the bees can build more honeycombs in them.

UTAH

Nickname: "Beehive State"

Capital: Salt Lake City

BUZZY BEE SALAD DRESSING

What you need:
- 4 tablespoons honey
- 3 tablespoons brown sugar
- 1 cup mayonnaise
- ½ teaspoon powdered ginger
- 3 tablespoons Dijon mustard
- Juice of 1 lemon
- 3 tablespoons soy sauce
- For salad: Washed lettuce and chopped vegetables of your choice (carrots, tomato, black olives, avocado, cucumber, onion, etc.)

What you do:

1. Put all dressing ingredients together in a medium bowl. Whisk together with a wire whisk until blended thoroughly.

2. Arrange lettuce and vegetables on a plate or bowl. Pour a small amount of dressing over the top of your salad and mix well, using salad tongs or 2 forks.

70

All trees produce sap, a clear juice that contains vitamins, minerals, and sugar. Sap rises from the roots and circulates throughout a tree, nourishing all its parts. Maple trees have unusually sweet sap. The sugar maple, one of more than 200 varieties of maples, has the sweetest sap of all.

Native Americans showed white settlers how to tap (that is, take sap from) sugar-maple trees. This was done in late winter, in the sugaring season, before the maples blossomed and the clear sap turned golden. Settlers soon learned to flavor their food with maple syrup (or boil it down to cakes of sugar to use later) like the Indians did.

Vermont's maple-syrup products are prized by gourmet cooks all over the world. Locals enjoy maple syrup in many regional dishes and, of course, on pancakes!

Nickname: "Green Mountain State"

Capital: Montpelier

VERMONT

NUTTY MAPLE BRITTLE

What you need:

- 1 cup maple syrup
- 1 tablespoon butter or margarine
- Candy thermometer
- 1 cup sliced almonds, peanuts, or walnut pieces

What you do:

1. Combine maple syrup and butter together in a saucepan and heat on low heat. Insert the candy thermometer into the syrup mixture until it reaches 290 degrees, or until a drop of the mixture separates into threads when you place it in cold water. The threads should be soft, not brittle.

2. Stir in nuts. Keep nuts submerged so they cook thoroughly. Keep stirring so the candy does not burn. Cook to 295 degrees on the candy thermometer.

3. Spread the mixture in a ¼-inch layer onto a nonstick cookie sheet.

4. Chill in the refrigerator until firm.

5. Break into pieces and enjoy!

Virginia is famous for salt-cured, country hams made from hogs that have been fed peanuts. Captain John Smith and the first permanent English settlers learned to make hams this way from the Indians they met when they first arrived in Virginia in 1607. Virginia hams have graced some of the finest tables in America and Europe: England's Queen Victoria insisted that Virginia hams be shipped regularly to London, while the famous actress Sarah Bernhardt demanded they be sent to her in Paris!

Nickname: "Old Dominion"

Capital: Richmond

VIRGINIA

SAUCY DOWN-HOME COUNTRY HAM

What you need:
- 2 tablespoons butter or margarine
- 4 precooked country ham slices, ¼- to ½-inch thick (preferably Virginia country ham!)
- ½ cup applesauce
- ¼ cup brown sugar
- 1 tablespoon lemon juice

What you do:
1. Melt the butter in a large skillet over low heat. Put the ham slices in the pan and cook the ham for 2 or 3 minutes on each side.

2. While the ham is cooking, mix the applesauce, brown sugar, and lemon juice in a small bowl. When the ham is done, spread the applesauce mixture on top of the ham. **Serves 4**

ABOUT BROWN SUGAR:

Brown sugar comes from the same sugarcane as white sugar. After white sugar is made, the leftover syrup is reboiled in a vacuum to produce a light or dark brown sugar. The darker the sugar, the stronger the flavor.

If brown sugar sits for very long, it can dry out and become hard. One solution: seal it in a jar with a slice of apple for a day or so. Another solution: seal it in a jar with a slice of slightly stale bread. After a while the bread will be hard as a rock. When that happens, replace it with another slightly stale piece of bread.

Munched a crisp, juicy apple lately? It may well have been from the fertile orchards of Washington, the United States' leading grower of apples. Although there's a saying, "as American as apple pie," apples are not a native American food. But they have been around a long time—since 1629, in fact, when the first American apple tree was planted in Massachusetts by one of that state's early governors.

Credit for starting many of America's early apple orchards goes to John Chapman, a colorful frontier nomad (wanderer) now remembered as Johnny Appleseed. Here's the story: Back in the pioneering days, Johnny took a walk (a long, long walk, lasting almost 50 years!) through what is now the Midwest, planting apple seeds wherever he found the right kind of soil.

Johnny lived out-of-doors and wore a rough flour sack for a shirt, nothing much for shoes, and an old cooking pot for a hat (he cooked in it, too!). He was kind to animals and generous to people, willing to share whatever he had (which was mostly apple seeds).

Nickname: "Evergreen State"

Capital: Olympia

WASHINGTON

JUICY BAKED APPLE TREAT

What you need:

- 4 red baking apples, washed
- 15–20 raisins
- 10 almonds
- 1 tablespoon cinnamon
- ½ cup hot water

What you do:

1. Preheat oven to 350 degrees.
2. Core apples (cut out the stem and inside seeds and seed pockets) without cutting out the bottom of the apple. You may need to ask an adult to help you with this.
3. Slit skin around the middle of each apple to prevent bursting.
4. Stuff each apple with 4–5 raisins, a couple of almonds, and sprinkle with cinnamon.
5. Put the apples in a baking dish. Fill each apple with water and pour the leftover water into the baking dish.
6. Bake for 30 minutes or until apples are soft inside.
7. When the apples have cooled, put them in small bowls and eat them with a knife and fork. They are great as a snack or dessert.

Dancers decked out in traditional Italian folk costumes swirl and sway on a stage in the center of the room. An accordion player dressed in green, white, and orange (the colors of Italy's flag) strolls among the tables. The mouthwatering aromas of spaghetti, lasagna, fettucine, and spicy pepperoni sausage fill the air. *Benvenuti* to West Virginia, home of the biggest Italian festival in America!

Italians immigrated to West Virginia by the thousands in the late 1800s and early 1900s, attracted by the promise of work in West Virginia's many coal mines. The work was steady and the pay was good, but the Italian coal miners missed their families and the customs and foods of the "old country." As soon as they saved enough money, they sent for their wives, brothers, sisters, cousins, parents, and best friends. Soon there were plenty of Italian cooks and dishes all over West Virginia!

WEST VIRGINIA

Nickname: "Mountain State"

Capital: Charleston

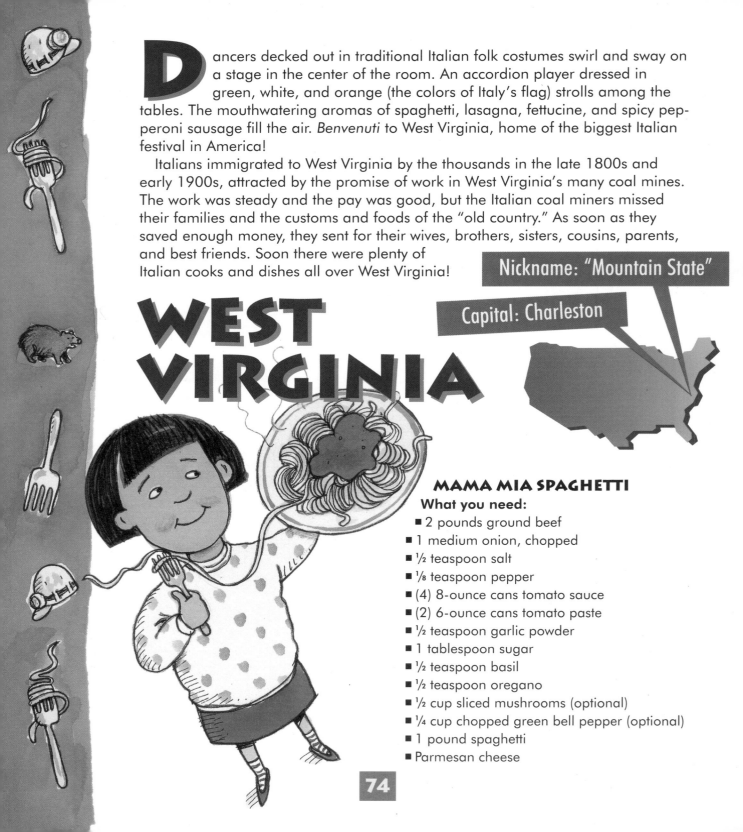

MAMA MIA SPAGHETTI
What you need:
- 2 pounds ground beef
- 1 medium onion, chopped
- ½ teaspoon salt
- ⅛ teaspoon pepper
- (4) 8-ounce cans tomato sauce
- (2) 6-ounce cans tomato paste
- ½ teaspoon garlic powder
- 1 tablespoon sugar
- ½ teaspoon basil
- ½ teaspoon oregano
- ½ cup sliced mushrooms (optional)
- ¼ cup chopped green bell pepper (optional)
- 1 pound spaghetti
- Parmesan cheese

GARLIC is added to almost all

Italian dishes. In addition to making food tasty, garlic helps people stay well! During the terrible plagues of Europe, some doctors stayed well by eating and wearing lots of garlic strung like beads on a necklace. Scientists still aren't sure whether the garlic really made those doctors immune to disease (that is, able to resist it), or whether they smelled so bad that everyone, including people with contagious germs, stayed far away!

Take two of these and call me in the morning!

What you do:

1. In a skillet on medium heat, cook the meat until browned. Using a wooden spoon, break apart the meat into small pieces while cooking.

2. Using a slotted spoon, remove the meat from the pan into a large saucepan.

3. To the large saucepan, add the onion, salt, pepper, tomato sauce, tomato paste, garlic powder, sugar, basil, and oregano. Mix well. Add mushrooms and bell peppers if desired.

4. Simmer on low heat, covered, for 1 hour. Stir occasionally.

5. Cook the spaghetti according to the package directions.

6. Serve spaghetti with sauce on top and sprinkle with Parmesan cheese.

Serves 12

West Virginia has mined more coal than any other state except Kentucky.

Why is Wisconsin known all over the world as "America's Dairyland"? Each year Wisconsin's 1.6 million dairy cows produce milk for 42 million people, butter for 68 million, and cheese for 86 million—which makes Wisconsin tops in milk, butter, and cheese production!

Milk is one of the most important foods in the world. Although it's mostly water, it's rich in carbohydrates and fats (for energy), protein (for growth), and vitamins and minerals (for muscles, teeth, and bones).

People have depended on milk in one form or another since the beginning of history. Foods made from milk, such as cheese, butter, and sour milk, were a big part of the diets of nomads who roamed the grasslands of Asia thousands of years ago. (Remember the Tartars? Flip back to Nebraska!) Most cheese is made by adding *rennet,* a liquid that comes from a calf's stomach, to fresh milk. Rennet causes milk to separate into white lumps (curd) and a watery liquid (whey). (Remember Little Miss Muffet, who sat on a tuffet, eating her curds and whey? Now you know what curds and whey are!) When the curd hardens, it becomes cheese.

Nickname: "America's Dairyland"

Capital: Madison

WISCONSIN

MOO SOUP

What you need:

- 3 tablespoons butter
- 1 large onion, chopped
- 1 stalk celery, chopped
- 2 medium carrots, peeled and chopped
- 3 tablespoons flour
- 1 ¾ cup beef broth
- 2 medium potatoes, peeled and cut into cubes
- 1 cup heavy cream
- 1 teaspoon nutmeg
- ⅛ teaspoon cayenne pepper
- Pinch of salt
- 3 cups (¾ pound) sharp cheddar cheese, grated

What you do:

1. In a large saucepan, stir-fry the first four ingredients until soft (4–5 minutes). Add the flour. Mix well and cook for 1 minute.

2. Add the beef broth a little bit at a time, stirring constantly until blended well.

3. Add the potatoes and bring to a boil.

4. Cover, turn the heat down to low, and simmer for 20 minutes, or until the potatoes are tender.

5. Carefully pour the mixture into a blender and puree. Return mixture to the pan. (You may want help from your adult assistant on this step.)

6. Add the cream and the seasonings (nutmeg, pepper, salt). Add cheese and simmer on low heat until the cheese is melted.

7. Pour soup into bowls and serve with crackers.

Mmooo, mmooo, good!

Wyoming is a land of wide-open spaces, where such cowboy words as *dogies, buckaroos, trail rides, stampedes, chowtime, chuckwagon,* and *rodeos* are still heard on the range. Hard-riding Wyoming cowboys need plenty of good grub to keep roping and riding. Stew hits the spot after a hard day in the saddle!

Nickname: "Cowboy State"

Capital: Cheyenne

WYOMING

COWBOY STEW

(Note: Ask for help with all the cutting in preparing this recipe.)

What you need:
- 2 cans tomato soup (undiluted)
- 2 cups water
- ½ cup flour
- 2 pounds beef, fat-trimmed, cut into 1-inch cubes
- 5 medium carrots, peeled and cut into 1-inch slices
- 1 large onion, chopped
- 6 medium potatoes, cut into 1 ½-inch chunks
- 4 celery stalks, cut into ½-inch pieces
- 4 beef bouillon cubes
- (1) 16-ounce package each of frozen peas and corn
- 1 teaspoon garlic powder
- Salt and pepper to taste

What you do:
1. Preheat oven to 275 degrees.
2. In a large saucepan, combine soup, water, and flour. Blend with a whisk until smooth.
3. Add the remaining ingredients to the soup mixture. Mix well.
4. Pour stew into a roasting pan.
5. Bake for 4–5 hours.

Find yourself a cowboy and have some stew. Serve with bread.

In 1869 women in Wyoming became the first females in the United States to be able to vote and hold public office. This earned Wyoming its other nickname: "Equality State."

JUST A REMINDER . . .

Nowadays, modern transportation makes it easy for Americans to visit other parts of the country on vacations. Changes in the way business is done mean more and more families are moving from state to state. As people travel back and forth and move here and there, they're taking recipes for their favorite traditional foods with them. As a result, Texas-style Mexican food is now popular in Ohio, just as Chicago-style deep-dish pizza is a favorite in Arizona. Cold-storage techniques mean that apples grown in Washington can be shipped and sold in Florida, while Florida oranges end up in Maryland.

So what does that mean? The foods featured for each state may represent regional favorites, but they are by no means enjoyed only in that state!

INDEX